# Reviews

Bryan consistently offers insightful and practical perspectives on a variety of evolving and demanding risk management issues. This book effectively exemplifies these qualities, making it a highly valuable resource for risk managers across all organisational settings.

– Patrick Barrett, Distinguished Honorary Professor
& Senior Fellow – ANCAAR
Research School of Accounting, ANU
Auditor-General of Australia 1995-2005

As the CEO of the RMIA, I am constantly seeking valuable resources to enhance the knowledge and skills of our members, and Bryan's blogs have proved to be an invaluable asset in this regard. Bryan can uniquely distil complex risk management concepts into actionable strategies and tangible steps. His writing style is clear, concise, and engaging, making it accessible to seasoned professionals and those new to the field.

Furthermore, I must commend Bryan for his commitment to consistency. Publishing a weekly blog year after year requires discipline, dedication, and a unique passion for sharing knowledge. Bryan has consistently delivered high-quality content, ensuring his readers have a steady stream of valuable insights to guide their risk management efforts.

– Simon Levy, CEO, Risk Management Institute
of Australasia (RMIA)

I have found Bryan's blogs a great resource assisting me in my professional development. The clarity, depth, and practicality of his insights have supported me to navigate and share risk concepts with others effectively. I highly recommend Bryan's blogs to anyone seeking a comprehensive and accessible discussion and thought on risk and risk management. Congratulations Bryan.

— **Andrew Booth, CRO, Cotton On Group**

I am a regular reader of Bryan's weekly blog and have found his musings on risk related topics to be insightful and thought provoking. The wide range of topics have allowed me to consider my challenges from a different perspective, often providing me with a more strategic lens through which to consider possible solutions.

— **David FitzGerald, Principal Risk Officer,**
**Department of Communities WA**

For all of us time poor professionals Bryan's weekly blogs give a bite sized morsel of risk insight with a distinctly commercial slant. Always thought provoking yet pragmatic, it's great to now have these compiled into one handy guide.

— **Claudia Bels FAICD, Non-Executive Director**
**Audit & Risk Committee Chair**

I have been a reader of Bryan's blogs for a few years now and have always found them a useful and concise reference resource. They are backed by his years of expertise working with a variety of businesses on risk management and strategy. He supports his blogs with some fantastic material, including whitepapers he has authored covering an array of topics, providing business management with practical and actionable advice. Bryan is also a great storyteller which he uses to good effect in supporting his blog messages.

– Lyall Bear, Business Advisor

Hey Bryan, just a thank you and a little feedback regarding these weekly blogs. I find them invaluable as they jog my memory of your book but also serve as a great way to cement good practice. I often find myself scrolling through past blogs before a meeting to best prepare myself and every time, I amend my delivery in some way to try to achieve a better outcome.

– Stuart Dixon, Senior Risk Specialist, Telstra

Bryan - these blogs that come through are great. There is always something topical that I take back to my organisation. Thank you for continuing to produce these - fantastic work.

– Daniel Dolatowski, Team Leader: Corporate Governance and Risk, City of Port Adelaide Enfield

Hi Bryan, I signed up to your blog as I recently took on a new role where I am responsible for operationalising a newly signed off RAS (the first one for a growing business), implementing new enterprise-wide risk management processes and setting it all up in a new system. Having come from a much bigger business with established frameworks and processes and a wide network for risk professionals to leverage off, I'm finding myself in need of additional resources. I'm finding your website and blog to be super helpful in accessing ERM resources as I work through some of the challenges I am encountering.

– Daria Hansen, Senior Risk Manager, Financial Services Industry

BRYAN'S BLOGS
From Blog to Book:
Years of Insights on Making Risk Stick

**Other books by the author:**

*DECIDE: How to Manage the Risk
in Your Decision Making*

*Persuasive Advising: How to Turn
Red Tape into Blue Ribbon*

*Risky Business: How Successful
Organisations Embrace Uncertainty*

# BRYAN'S BLOGS

From Blog to Book
Years of Insights on Making Risk Stick

BRYAN WHITEFIELD

Published by Bryan Whitefield Consulting
PO Box 7367 Warringah Mall
Brookvale NSW 2100 Australia

www.bryanwhitefield.com

First published July, 2023

ISBN: 978-0-9945218-8-0

NATIONAL LIBRARY OF AUSTRALIA    A catalogue record for this
book is available from the
National Library of Australia

Cover design by Ignite Creative
Typesetting by BookPOD
Printed by IngramSpark

# About the Author

Bryan Whitefield is a management consultant in the fields of risk, influence and team decision making. His love for solving complex situations was fuelled at the start of his career by his studies in chemical engineering, when quite by chance he 'fell into' the field of risk. Since then he has earned a reputation as the go-to guy for demystifying the role and function of risk management in organisations, helping key decision makers value risk management and the risk profession.

Bryan is the author of *DECIDE: How to Manage the Risk in Your Decision Making*; *Persuasive Advising: How to Turn Red Tape into Blue Ribbon* and *Risky Business: How Successful Organisations Embrace Uncertainty* (Amazon Best Seller). He was President and Chair of the RMIA from 2013 through 2015. Licensed by the RMIA as a Certified Chief Risk Officer (CCRO), since 2019 he is the designer and facilitator of their flagship Enterprise Risk Management Course.

To learn more about Bryan visit www.bryanwhitefield.com. Additionally, all the links throughout this book can be found at https://www.bryanwhitefield.com.au/blog-book-links/ or via this QR code:

# Acknowledgements

For more than two decades I have had the privilege of working as a risk management consultant, assisting organisations and their leaders across various industries, in navigating the ever-changing landscape of uncertainty. I have witnessed the transformative power of risk management when approached with diligence, inclusiveness and an open mind.

Throughout this journey I have documented my reflections, insights and resources in my blogs, sharing the wisdom gained from countless interactions with professionals who strive to turn challenges into opportunities. This book encapsulates the last three years of my weekly written blogs, showcasing my experiences and top tips, offering practical advice, case studies and thought-provoking conversations on a wide range of risk-related topics. Whether you are a seasoned risk professional, a business leader, or simply someone interested in learning more of the benefits of risk management, I believe you will find value within these pages.

Keep in mind, this book is not a comprehensive manual of risk management techniques, nor is it a crystal ball to predict the future. Instead, it is a reflection of my observations and lessons learned over the years. It is an invitation to embrace uncertainty, to take risks eyes-wide-open to seize opportunities, and to develop a mindset that enables you to navigate uncharted territories with confidence and agility.

And finally, I would like to express my deepest gratitude to all my readers and clients who have supported me throughout my career. Your feedback, engagement and shared experiences have been instrumental in shaping my understanding of risk management and how best I can serve you all. I dedicate this book to you, with the hope that it will be a source of inspiration and empowerment in your own risk management journeys.

Cheers
Bryan

# Contents

## RISK ASSESSMENT

## MASTERING RISK WORKSHOP FACILITATION

# KPI | KRI

## QUANTIFICATION

## INDUSTRY DISRUPTION

## LEADERSHIP

## SCENARIO PLANNING

# List of Figures

# ENTERPRISE RISK MANAGEMENT

# It's Time
2 February 2021

It's time we did something about the persistent perception of risk as a compliance function. Something that is done to keep the board, the audit and risk committee or a regulator happy. Another task in addition to running a successful organisation.

**STOP.** *Before you decide that risk is valued in your organisation.* Ask yourself if the executive simply say they know and believe in the importance of the risk function or if they truly utilise the outputs from risk processes in their decision making. Is risk an afterthought or is good risk assessment demanded at the right times for the right reasons?

**LOOK.** *Before you cast blame.* Look at your risk function and ask if what they are doing and how they are doing it is valuable to an executive team. Are they providing real insights to improve decision making? Is the information communicated in a clear, concise and timely manner?

**LISTEN.** *Before you move on.* Go and speak to key stakeholders of the risk function and ask them what they value and what they don't. Listen carefully for the word "but". Are they really happy to attend the next meeting with the risk team?

Yes, it's time we elevated the risk function in organisations, however, more importantly it's time we fixed ineffective approaches to the management of risk in organisations.

And that is why I have written *Risky Business: How Successful Organisations Embrace Uncertainty*. It is a book for senior leaders, risk practitioners and others interested in ensuring their organisation embraces uncertainty. That risk management is used to take calculated risk, eyes wide open, bringing all stakeholders along the way.

Cheers
Bryan

Organisations need to embrace uncertainty because of the Uncertainty Paradox, which states that the only certainty is uncertainty. No one can predict the future. This is the first concept I explore in my new book *Risky Business: How Successful Organisations Embrace Uncertainty.*

The most successful organisations learn to systematically confront and get comfortable with uncertainty. They learn to embrace it. They face the drivers of their uncertainty, one by one. Those they can proactively manage, they do. When they can't, they put in place a 'Plan B' to manage the fallout if the worst happens. Rather than simply managing what hurt in the past by adding another process over another process, the organisation looks to identify its fears and systematically work through them. It ignores none of them, it lives with each of them and so has a clearer view of them.

While this is what we were forced to do as COVID hit, it is what successful organisations do as a matter of course. And the evidence is clear that those who did this best were advanced in their implementation of enterprise risk management. In his paper titled *COVID-19 Makes a Strong Business Case for Enterprise Risk Management,*

Robert van der Meulen found that "an agile response occurred far more often when clear processes already existed."

Taken to the nth degree you have the Elon Musks of the world. So driven, so passionate, they stare down the fear.

Stay safe!

Cheers
Bryan

# Risk-Speak Is $#!t-Speak

23 February 2021

I have long complained that the risk profession has made risk management needlessly complex. Part of it is the creation of our own language. Risk-speak. We put "risk" in front of or after perfectly normal words like conduct, appetite and reputation.

By putting risk in front of or behind these words we feel we create an important emphasis for leaders. Worse still, when we really get going with all our jargon it's like we are speaking Parseltongue, the language of serpents in the imaginary world of Harry Potter.

The result is we *separate risk from the world of business*. We have become an add-on. Something that must be done in addition to running a successful business.

Your focus must be on integrating risk into business-as-usual. Concentrate on blending good risk management principles into existing practices. Take procurement for example. The need for and approach to assessing risk for a procurement should be created and owned by the procurement function. By all means support them but let them design it into their framework and systems because they will know how best to do so while minimising red tape.

There are more tips on defeating risk-speak in my new book _Risky Business: How Successful Organisations Embrace Uncertainty._

Stay safe!

Cheers
Bryan

# We've Been Creeping Towards It for Decades
## 2 March 2021

I had my book launch for _Risky Business: How Successful Organisations Embrace Uncertainty_ on Thursday afternoon. What a fantastic afternoon with near on two hundred risk professionals, current and past clients and friends and family helping me to celebrate.

This is an important book for the risk profession and organisations alike. As I said during my presentation, the time for change is now. The time for the risk profession to step up is now.

During the event I showed the figure below. I explained how I had observed businesses creeping from treating risk as a compliance activity, to one where it is valued for the insights it brings and the leadership it provides in determining the type and amount of risk to take. This means moving business leaders from treating risk as tick and flick add-on, to a position where they welcome the support of the risk team and hold themselves accountable for managing uncertainty.

I took a poll of the audience with the results broadly indicative of my experience in working with organisations and risk practitioners. Pleasantly just over 50% said their organisation was operating above the line in the 2010s or

*I was asked what the 2030s would look like for risk management. My answer? Business leaders will be accountable and the risk profession will have a seat at the table where the decisions are made.*

2020s with just over 20% in the 2020s. Sadly, almost 50% are not treating risk as valuable, with 14% in the 1990s.

The poll emphasises that the time for the risk profession is now. During the 2020s we must shift 80% of organisations to the point where business leaders are taking accountability for risk. To do this, you must have a focus on building the influence of you and your risk team. The more you can create excellent analysis and translate it into excellent advice actioned by management, the sooner leaders will look forward to working with you and be willing to hold themselves accountable.

| DECADE | RISK THEME | BUSINESS LEADERSHIP | RISK LEADERSHIP |
|--------|-----------|---------------------|-----------------|
| 2020s | Leadership | Be Accountable | Influence |
| 2010s | Insights | Look Forward | Analytics |
| 2000s | Comfort | Be Prepared | Assurance |
| 1990s | Compliance | Tick & Flick | Training |

Figure 1: Risk Management Through the Decades

At the Q&A at the end of the launch I was asked what the 2030s would look like for risk management. My answer? Business leaders will be accountable and the risk profession will have a seat at the table where the decisions are made.

The last chapter of *Risky Business: How Successful Organisations Embrace Uncertainty* is on persuasive advising so please grab a copy if you have not earned yourself a free one as yet. And if you want to go deep on influence, check out my Persuasive Adviser Program.

Stay safe and keep on building your influence!

Cheers
Bryan

*An organisation
is a complex
system. It can't be
controlled. It can
only be influenced.*

# Working Within a Complex System
## 6 March 2021

Aaron Dignan, in an excerpt from his book *Brave New Work* on 'Changing Organisational Mindset' explains the difference between complicated and complex by comparing it to the difference between a car and traffic.[1] Everything about a car has been worked out by scientists and engineers and how it moves is predictable. We can't predict precisely how traffic will move despite our best modelling efforts.

Dignan explains that complex systems are more about 'relationships and interactions among their components than about the components themselves. And these interactions give rise to unpredictable behaviour.'

Now think about your organisation. Can you predict with certainty the behaviours you see? No. An organisation is a complex system. It can't be controlled. It can only be influenced.

Dignan goes on to explain that despite our best attempts to control an organisation through policy, process and system, it proves impossible. We end up with plenty

---

1   Dignan, Aaron. 'Changing Organisational Mindset', *Stanford Social Innovation Review*, March 18, 2019. https://ssir.org/books/excerpts/entry/changing_ organizational_mindset

of rules or constraints, which creates friction and organisational drag. The way to nurture the culture of an organisation, he argues, is to create the right conditions for individual decision makers to find a way to achieve organisational goals.

Therein lies the secret of good risk management. While we live and preach a world of controls, be assured, you can't control the organisation as a whole. Only some of its components. You need to step back and take a big picture view of the organisation and work on influencing behaviours until there is a collective consciousness that is reflected in the organisation's culture. One that results in leaders applying risk-based decision making in pursuit of objectives.

In my book *Risky Business: How Successful Organisations Embrace Uncertainty,* Chapter 4 is titled The Agents of Complexity. In it I explain how regulators, stock market analysts, government ministers and many others are agents that create complexity. And I highlight some of the ways to deal with them by influencing their views and approach. Speaking of influencing, check out my Persuasive Adviser Program.

Stay safe and keep on building your influence!

Cheers
Bryan

# The End Game for Risk
16 March 2021

Chapter 5 of my book *Risky Business: How Successful Organisations Embrace Uncertainty* is titled The End Game. Whenever I run workshops with senior leaders, I always make sure they understand what they should be looking to achieve from their investment in risk management. Otherwise, they might think it is just "good governance" and go about ticking the box while getting on with the important business of running the organisation. However, the end game might not be what you first think.

I have frequently talked about resilience as being one of the benefits of a great strategy and sound risk management. For example, here is a paper I wrote about selling resilience. These days when I mention resilience to executives I start with this question:

"What makes a small business resilient?"

The answer is "agility". The ability to move faster than the giant sloths with stellar balance sheets. These days in the world of start-ups, I have no problem giving my audience a relevant example. Then I set them straight on what they should be seeking from their risk program.

The target must be agility. And the means is through

*Yes, we all make mistakes. However, risk done well means minimal effort resulting in better decisions.*

faster, better decision making within the organisation's appetite for risk. That is the end game for risk. Where decision makers in organisations take into account the uncertainty surrounding themselves and their objectives, resulting in less stuff ups and the resultant rework. And if decision making remains within the organisation's appetite for risk, the stuff ups are not too damaging.

Yes, we all make mistakes. However, risk done well means minimal effort resulting in better decisions. Keeping in mind, risk done well is not overly complex and has minimal red tape.

Unfortunately, not too many risk programs are designed with simplicity or minimal in mind.

Stay safe!

Cheers
Bryan

# Checklist Designers

23 March 2021

One of the worst insults you can throw at a risk practitioner is that you are merely a "checklist designer". Chapter 6 of my book *Risky Business: How Successful Organisations Embrace Uncertainty* is titled Designing Success. When I run the RMIA's Enterprise Risk Management program we discuss the level of maturity of the organisations that participants work in using the scale from "compliance" to "leadership" as I described in this recent blog, 'We've been creeping towards it for decades.' And then we discuss the level of influence a practitioner has in organisations at various levels of maturity. And the lowest level of influence is in organisations that treat risk as a compliance activity which makes the risk team simply "checklist designers".

One step up are organisations that require risk to provide "comfort" to the audit and risk committee or the board or a regulator. The risk team is then seen as "framework designers". Look no further than these quotes from the APRILA report into the culture in CBA to reinforce the perceptions of some risk teams as checklist or framework designers:

- "... over 100 respondents expressed the sentiment that risk management activities are 'onerous', 'complex', 'time consuming', and 'really achieves very little other than as a form filling exercise.'"

- "The risk function was also described as focusing on policy writing and correctness of frameworks over implementation and engagement with the business."

Ironically, framework design is critical to growing a strong risk culture. The problem is that many, many designs are overly complex, overly onerous and overly long! If you want to design a great framework, grab a copy of my book and come to the next RMIA ERM course!

Stay safe!

Cheers
Bryan

PS. I'm thrilled to say my book *Risky Business: How Successful Organisations Embrace Uncertainty* hit the #1 Amazon Best Seller list this week in the Risk Management Category. If you have read it and think it's worthy of a review, I would greatly appreciate your time in leaving one here. You would make this risk nerd very, very happy.

# Designing Experiences
30 March 2021

I like to think that when I work with boards, executive teams and other teams that they are buying an experience, as much as my knowledge of the topic at hand. That is, they feel engaged.

Last week on my blog 'Checklist Designers', I emphasised the need to design great risk frameworks. The next bit of advice I give in Chapter 6 of my book *Risky Business: How Successful Organisations Embrace Uncertainty*, titled Designing Success, is to give your audience a fantastic first experience of the new or revised framework. That is, you need to design a fantastic first experience of the framework to knock down any misperceptions that the framework is too long, onerous or complex.

The following are a couple of examples of what not to do, and what to do, to give a good experience of a new framework:

- Don't put the framework up on the internet with a policy signed by the CEO.
- Do sit down with each area of the business individually to work through the why, how and what of the framework.
- Don't start with risk reporting.

- Do start with risk insights to teams, beginning with the executive.

To make sure I can give a team really good insights into the risks they are facing I follow a well-rehearsed formula of:

- Preparing – what I do before a workshop. I use analysis tools to gain insight.
- Facilitating – what I do in a workshop. I use a variety of techniques to create insight.
- Sensemaking – what I do after a workshop. I use a simple process to help the team check that the insights are valid, in the clear light of day, outside of the workshop.

If you want to know more about some of these techniques, do grab a copy of my book or come to my next Mastering Risk Workshop Facilitation course which covers each of these three steps in depth!

Stay safe!

Cheers
Bryan

# Design Success – Kill TLM and Adopt T-PM

6 April 2021

**Kill the Three Lines Model** and **adopt** what I call the **Tri-Partite Model of Risk**! In a nutshell, the essence of T-PM is:

- Business decision makers are **wholly** accountable for the **decisions they make.**
- The risk function is only responsible for providing advice but is **wholly** accountable for the **quality of that advice.**
- The assurance function is **wholly** accountable for assessing the **effectiveness of the two working together.**

This is what is necessary to design success for your risk function and to be part of the momentum shift, moving risk from being seen as a painful compliance activity to being seen as *valuable.*

And can I tell you, this momentum shift can't arrive too soon. Just last weekend I was on a golf trip with 11 buddies. The partner of one of my friend's had recently joined one of the big banks in risk and compliance. When one of the other guys heard this he remarked "Man, I can't believe anyone can like doing that s#!t."

*Once friends sit down
and discuss with
me my philosophy
about risk-taking in
organisations, they
get it. But it takes
more than a minute
for them to get it.*

Yep, this is what I've had to put up with for decades. Once friends sit down and discuss with me my philosophy about risk-taking in organisations, they get it. But it takes more than a minute for them to get it.

If you want a full explanation of what I call the Tri-Partite Model of Risk, then download Chapter 7: Designing Success from my book *Risky Business: How Successful Organisations Embrace Uncertainty*. If you want to read about all the reasons we should kill off the Three Lines Model, previously the Three Lines of Defence Model, then you can buy the book here.

Stay safe!

Cheers
Bryan

# Delivering Instant Success
13 April 2021

Sorry. No such thing when it comes to Change Programs like implementing your risk framework. Ask any professional change manager. And they don't teach a lot of change management at risk school, do they? Haha! What risk school?

Most risk people get technical training. Few, as I have pointed out before in my blog, _We must cure Mollisvitaephobia_, get sufficient training in soft skills which are essential to effect change. On top of that, risk departments are also short on resources. After all, aren't you just this necessary cost centre? So, what should you do if you need to affect a major Change Program, you are not an expert in change management and you are short on resources?

As I recommend in my book _Risky Business: How Successful Organisations Embrace Uncertainty_, you need to build a Change Program that results in there being advocates for risk within business units. Risk champions is another name for them, or a risk community of practice.

Forming, engaging and building engagement between communities of practice and the risk function is one of my favourite challenges. I love turning good, smart, business-savvy subject matter experts (SMEs) in to good, smart, business savvy SMEs that are good at managing uncertainty. They become the people who say, "Hey team, I think this is one we should stop and have a think about a bit more." And proceed to facilitate a wee risk assessment or call in the experts from risk to run a more in-depth risk workshop.

If you want to know more about building advocates so that risk moves from being seen as the "Department of No" to the "Department of Grow" then download Chapter 7: Designing Success from my book *Risky Business: How Successful Organisations Embrace Uncertainty*. If you want to get my broader take on challenges facing the risk profession and my proposed solutions, you can buy the book here.

Stay safe!

Cheers
Bryan

# Great Frameworks: Another Bigger Is Not Better

22 June 2021

When I run training for the development of risk frameworks, I ask participants to hold up their hand if they have a framework that is more than a couple of pages. I ask them to keep their hand up if it's more than 10 pages, 20, 50 and I keep going if needs be. The winner so far had a framework that was over 200 pages. I kid you not. No wonder they were there to get help.

A great risk framework achieves your desired goals in the least amount of words possible. It should:

- Integrate risk into business-as-usual.
- Show risk to be an enabler of success.
- Be able to be overviewed and comprehended in 15 minutes.

Does yours? If not, here is a tip. Break it up.

I break up risk frameworks into Policy, Guideline and Procedure. The policy gives the "why" and sets the direction the organisation needs to head. The guideline contains the "what" and acts like a roadmap for the integration of risk into business-as-usual. And the procedure provides the "how", the instructions for risk assessment and escalation as required.

The policy is a page or 3. The guideline, say 3 to 8 pages. And the procedure is as long as it needs to be to provide instructions. Maybe 8 to 10, including templates, if you don't have a training package that provides staff with a guided tour through the risk assessment and reporting processes.

If you want to know more about framework design, download _Chapter 7: Designing Success_ of my book _Risky Business: How Successful Organisations Embrace Uncertainty_ and view more of my insights on my website here. Better still, you can sign up for the RMIA's Enterprise Risk Management course and go into framework development in detail.

Stay safe!

Cheers
Bryan

# It's What We Do
29 June 2021

A key goal for the design of any organisational framework should be to integrate it into business-as-usual. So that it is simply "how things are done around here". Especially for a risk framework.

Risk management, not risk taking, still suffers from an abundance of misperception of it being a compliance activity. Something that has to be done as an extra and not really related to "real work".

Last week on my blog 'Great Frameworks: Another Bigger is not Better', I gave a tip on how to make your risk framework easily digestible by a leader so they take the time to understand its value. My number one tip for integrating risk into business-as-usual is to integrate performance and risk reporting. Such that, a leader reports on their performance and the risk to future performance, all in one breath so to speak.

Too often I see risk reporting only occurring because the risk team made contact. What follows is delays in getting information back, followed by postponement of the meetings in which risk was to be discussed. By the time the discussion is had, everything is pretty much old news and of little value.

*Risk management, not risk taking, still suffers from an abundance of misperception of it being a compliance activity. Something that has to be done as an extra and not really related to "real work".*

Still, at least they can say we "ticked the box" on that one!

Stay safe!

Cheers
Bryan

# Enable Your Success

6 July 2021

You have probably heard the risk function being called an enabling function. Because it is. It helps the main producing areas of the business to be more successful. When I present to executive teams to give them a picture of enterprise risk management, the first thing I do is dispel any hint of the myth that risk is a compliance function. I stress early, and often, that they should engage with the risk program to be successful! Not to avoid bad things happening.

I go on to plead with them to do as much risk management as is needed to be successful. Not too much or too little. Too much means unnecessary red tape and a drag on the business. Too little and you will be held back by too many surprises.

When designing your enterprise risk framework, you should focus on showing risk as an enabler, not a compliance function. A big part of that is by integrating risk into business-as-usual which I wrote about on my blog 'It's what we do' last week. However, even more importantly, you need to ensure risk is seen as enabling faster and better decision making. I do this by focusing in on:

- **Knowledge** – Managing risk means making

decisions based on the best information available. This means the communication of information up and down the organisational hierarchy and across silos.

- **Decisions** – Decisions by default are always made under a degree of uncertainty, otherwise a decision would not be required. While all our decisions should consider risk, some decisions need more attention than others. Focus in on the decisions that matter!

- **Support** – We all have unconscious bias. The risk function helps decision makers manage this, by supporting with insights, the decisions that matter.

- **Culture** – Behaviours don't lie. Your framework should be clear on the risk-taking behaviours that are appropriate for the success of your organisation.

Focus on these four areas in the design and implementation of your risk framework and you will be enabling your success.

Stay safe!

Cheers
Bryan

# Synthesise Your Framework

13 July 2021

Last week I had leadership expert Ingrid Messner present on Wise Leadership to my Risk Leadership group. One of her leadership tips on influencing stakeholders was to apply systems thinking. To develop a mental model of all the pieces of the puzzle that are influencing a person and the decisions they need to make.

The tip immediately reminded me of the benefit of a system map when designing a framework. So that you are clear on the other frameworks, systems and processes your framework needs to integrate with, to ensure managing risk is part of business-as-usual. I wrote about this two weeks ago in *It's what we do.*

The three key tools I use to obtain sufficient context to develop a mental model (or system map) of how decisions are made in an organisation are:

- Stakeholder analysis – Identifies who will be impacted and how significant that is.
- PESTLE analysis – Identifies externalities the framework will need to address.
- Capability analysis – Identifies internal challenges and opportunities for the design of the framework.

You can access samples and templates for these tools via my <u>resources section</u> of my website.

Ingrid was also encouraging the group to use more of their body in understanding their influencing challenge. Another tip she gave us was to write the various nodes of the system map on pieces of paper and place them on the floor, for us then to step into the middle of them and look at the nodes. The act of stepping in and looking around creates a new perspective.

And I can assure you, we need a different perspective on frameworks if we are going to lift our game in the risk profession.

Stay safe!

Cheers
Bryan

# Intelligent Risk Taking
20 July 2021

Next week I am hosting a roundtable discussion on the future of risk frameworks. I am uncertain as to what may be discovered, however, what I do know is that the topic is of interest. The seats filled fast, and I had a number of my readers send me a note about it, some who could not make the event sent me their thoughts.

One was my Danish colleague <u>Hans Læssøe.</u> He sent me a short paper he authored making the case for dispensing with the risk management function all together. In essence, a situation where all staff understand the need to address uncertainty in their business and take actions to do so.

Let's see where the roundtable discussion takes us, however for now risk management is here to stay. So let me share a few of the most important points that Hans makes in the paper that I also make in my book *Risky Business: How Successful Organisations Embrace Uncertainty*:

1. Risk management (coordinated activities to manage risk) is happening everywhere in the business. However, it is not necessarily called that. See my blog titled <u>It's what we do</u>. Don't recreate the wheel. Only look to improve it if it

is not working rather than making sure the word "risk" be used.

2. We can't keep doing the same thing over and over and expect a better result. Hence my criticism of the industry and regulators for trying for decades to implement the Three Lines of Defence (now the Three Lines Model). Its design has a few fundamental flaws that go against human nature and I expand on this and more in Chapter 4: Agents of Complexity.

3. We need to put more quantification into our analysis of risk. See my blog Solving Quantifornication.

4. The need to ensure the management of risk is focused on the business and specifically enhancing performance of the business in pursuit of objectives. Or as Hans so nicely puts it:

"... the focus of risk management automatically changes from being risk centric and risk averse to being objective centric and focused on optimised/ intelligent risk taking.'"

Thanks Hans and keep up the great work.

Stay safe!

Cheers
Bryan

# Timely Horizons
1 June 2021

Reading the signals indicating your organisation is on-track or off-track (see <u>Reading the tea leaves</u>, <u>Heading them off at the pass</u>, <u>KRISS or KISS</u>) needs to be considered across three time horizons, in order to make your KPIs and KRIs "timely".

My colleague Dr Andrew Pratley introduced me to the Three Horizons of Growth concept introduced by Mehrdad Baghai, Lar Bradshaw, Stephen Coley and David White in their 1999 paper in the Journal of Business Strategy[2]. Their thesis was that in order to sustain growth, you need to be monitoring which parts of the business are in mature, emergent and embryonic phases and that you need to keep feeding the growth pipeline with new products and services as existing ones fade away.

In the diagram over the page I take their lead and show the difference between the horizons in terms of risk. The implication is the type of risk assessment you will do, how often and to what end. For example, you don't need to be assessing emerging risk as frequently as your day-to-day risks or risks to implementation of your strategy. But you should think about them from time to time - and

---

2    Baghai, M., Bradshaw, L., Coley, S., & White, D. (1999). Performance measures Calibrating for growth. Journal of Business Strategy, 20(4), 17-21.

*Embracing
uncertainty is
opportunity.
Leading you to
take opportunities
others don't know
about or have not
yet developed the
capability to do so.*

more frequently - the more dynamic or disrupted your industry.

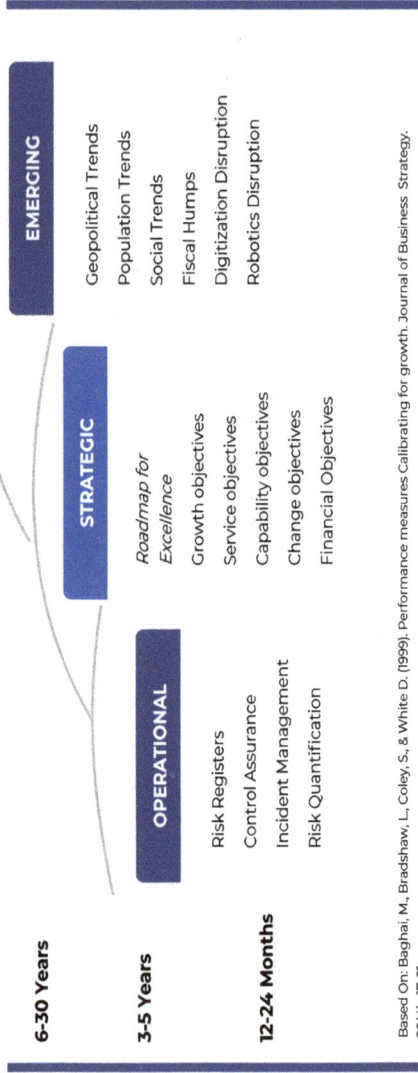

| | 6-30 Years | 3-5 Years | 12-24 Months |
|---|---|---|---|
| | **EMERGING** | **STRATEGIC** | **OPERATIONAL** |
| | Geopolitical Trends | *Roadmap for Excellence* | Risk Registers |
| | Population Trends | Growth objectives | Control Assurance |
| | Social Trends | Service objectives | Incident Management |
| | Fiscal Humps | Capability objectives | Risk Quantification |
| | Digitization Disruption | Change objectives | |
| | Robotics Disruption | Financial Objectives | |

**Figure 2: Risk Across Three Time Zones**

Based On: Baghai, M., Bradshaw, L., Coley, S., & White D. (1999). Performance measures Calibrating for growth. Journal of Business Strategy. 20(4), 17-21.

The next step is to identify the KPIs and KRIs that you should review each time you turn your mind to each horizon. They are very different and more obscure for emerging risks than for your day-to-day operational ones.

One thing is for sure. It re-emphasises for me that uncertainty is a strategic leader's best friend. Embracing uncertainty is opportunity. Leading you to take opportunities others don't know about or have not yet developed the capability to do so.

To read more on Time Horizons you can download Chapter 9: Reading the Signals from my book *Risky Business: How Successful Organisations Embrace Uncertainty*. Better still, buy my book and gain access to free resources that are there to help organisations perform better, faster!

Cheers
Bryan

# Summary in Detail

28 September 2021

I got the term "summary in detail" from a fantastic client of mine who I worked with for near on a decade. We were presenting a risk profile in a meeting and at one end of the table someone was complaining about the amount of detail. At the other end of the table someone was wanting to know more, to dig deeper.

At the end of the meeting, I turned to him and in a sort of frustrated tone said: "At one end of the table they wanted less detail and at the other end they wanted more!" His reply: "Welcome to my world, everyone wants summary in detail!"

A couple of years earlier, in 2007, I was working with a large government agency in Canberra. I helped them develop a bottom-up strategic risk profile. When it was time to report to the executive on the risk profile, I was not required at the meeting and was told they needed to have all the risks on one page. I said: "No worries about me not being at the meeting, but you'll 'get smashed' if you just provide a list of the top risks."

They did not take my advice and they got smashed. Why? Because there was no context for the executive. And, because they wanted the risk profile developed bottom-up, the executive's views on what senior leaders should be concerned about had not been considered.

Since then, I have made it a firm policy that whenever presenting a risk profile to an executive team or board, it must never be presented as a mere list of risks on a page. Instead, it should be accompanied by a comprehensive summary that follows the timeless adage of "What, So What, and Now What." This approach ensures that context is provided, enabling them to understand the significance of the risks, their implications, and the necessary actions or endorsements required.

Now back to the summary in detail meeting. My takeaway from that day was, that even if you provide context, there will always be some who want more and some who want less and so you need to accommodate both ends of the spectrum.

From then onwards I set-up my MS Excel risk profile template to facilitate the unveiling of risk information from a high level, to provide more detail. I've never had the same situation since.

Luckily for you, modern risk management applications facilitate summary in detail much more effectively and efficiently than a spreadsheet. Hence why I was very pleased to partner with Camms to run this webinar on risk reporting and the provision of "Summary in Detail."

Stay safe!

Cheers
Bryan

*Organisations that have a low level of maturity when it comes to risk-based decision making have a lot of untapped potential.*

# Immaturity Provides Opportunity
28 September 2021

Organisations that have a low level of maturity when it comes to risk-based decision making have a lot of untapped potential. The explanation is in the tag line to my latest book *Risky Business: How Successful Organisations Embrace Uncertainty.* Developing a strong capability and culture of risk-based decision-making lets organisations take on more risk and achieve greater success. It just makes sense. The question is how many of the more formal risk management practices of risk registers, risk workshops, control testing, culture assessments and the like are needed to achieve it.

Consider my model of risk maturity shown in **Figure 3: Risk Maturity Curve.** There are five levels of risk maturity tracking from Vulnerable to Agile. The overarching concept is that an organisation with a high level of risk maturity is more agile because staff at all levels of the organisation understand the risk associated with their environment, understand the board's appetite for risk taking and can make decisions effectively and promptly.

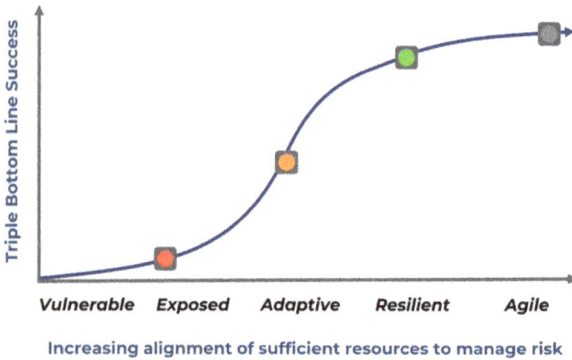

Figure 3: Risk Maturity Curve

Many people will say the aim of risk management is to create resilience. With my model the aim is to achieve resilience and move beyond that to become more agile. When I engage with senior executives of large organisations on enterprise risk, I ask them what makes a small business resilient. The answer they discover is agility i.e. its ability to adapt like so many have had to do these past 18 months just to survive. What I offer them is an ability to regain the agility they once had when they were a smaller, fast-growing organisation.

However, to deliver agility, the organisation's approach to risk must be to minimise red tape to ensure it maximises insights into decision-making, within a well-understood appetite for risk.

As can be seen in **Figure 3**. The use of an s-curve shows that to move from Exposed to Resilient can be done quite rapidly. Moving beyond Resilient to Agility has diminishing returns for the effort expended. And that is why organisations must carefully choose optimum levels of formal risk management. Too much and it becomes organisational drag. Too little and opportunities are missed while costly mistakes are being untangled.

You can check out more information on risk maturity here as well as my risk maturity model where you can take a short, 10 question self-assessment to place your organisation on my maturity curve.

Stay safe!

Cheers
Bryan

# Impact Value
8 March 2022

I tried something different last week. I posted a "musing" on LinkedIn. It was an excerpt from my book *Risky Business: How Successful Organisations Embrace Uncertainty* that read:

> "Risk management isn't rocket science. It's about managing uncertainty.
>
> And, done well, it delivers real value for organisations."

It sparked quite a lot of activity including some discussion on how to value the risk function.

Here are a couple of my replies on the topic:

To Norman Marks:

"Re the value of ERM, I have found some limited academic research (see references below) on the value of ERM that does show a correlation between good ERM practices and firm value – however my usual answer is along the lines of yours. Like Internal Audit, the fact senior leaders invest in it and appreciate the service being provided is evidence of value."

References:

Hoty, Robert E., and Liebenberg, Andrew P. 'Evidence of the Value of Enterprise Risk Management', Journal of Applied Corporate Finance, vol. 27, no. 1, Winter 2015.

Lechner, Philipp, and Gatzert, Nadine. 'Determinants and Value of Enterprise Risk Management: Empirical Evidence from Germany', European Journal of Finance, vol. 24, no. 10, 2018

AND

To Sabrina Segal:

"Thanks for asking the eternal question. I usually start off with something like "that's easy" and soon start talking about running your organisation in an alternate universe alongside this one. People get that it is not easy.

If you have a look at the post from Norman Marks on in this thread, I commented about value – so you could as a minimum quote that academic research.

Another approach you could take is to develop a decision register (Richard Thaler recommends this in his book *Nudge* I think). For each decision, the level/quality of consideration of risk would need to be assessed. You would do this across a range of governance committees and over time you should see a pattern develop.

Other than that, focus on delivering value, earning trusted adviser status and what you need should be provided.

Good luck!"

Two observations. Firstly, there were lots of comments about how difficult it is to tangibly measure the value of the risk function. Secondly, it is a universal challenge. Norman is in the US and Sabrina is in Egypt.

As always, I'd be interested to hear your views.

Stay safe and make change.

Cheers
Bryan

# Expectations Management
20 September 2022

I'm back from a wonderful six-week trip to Canada and the US visiting family and friends. As always, I like to write a blog about risk management from the experiences I have when on holiday. Some of our activities had a risk element to them, for example, boat camping in northern British Columbia and taking bear spray with us to "go up the hill" to the loo, in case we met a black bear – or worse – a grizzly! As I sit here reflecting, I find myself writing about Expectations Management.

Travel has been in the media, social media and in many a conversation over the last few months. And many, including the airlines, have been doing plenty of expectation management, albeit after poor performance earlier when things got busy again. We even got an email from the CEO of Air Canada in June saying they were cancelling some flights now for July and August because they became certain they would not be able to meet the published schedule. We had been warned.

And so we embarked on nine separate flights with checked baggage. Six of them international involving customs and immigration. The outcome? No lost bags and every flight (bar one) was pretty much on time. The delayed one was only about an hour or so late and most of our line ups for security and customs were way less than an hour. Did we spend a little more time sitting in airports because we got through faster? Yes. Did we care? No, plenty to do these days with streaming, books and people-watching in countries we'd been unable to visit for a couple of years. Things change in that time, especially from a pandemic!

As a risk guy, I look at pretty much everything through a risk lens. And so I see expectations management as simply good risk management. Turn that on its head and any businessperson worth a dollar or more knows risk management is simply good management. The management of uncertainty. And the best of the best embrace uncertainty to achieve more, out compete and deliver a legacy.

For more on embracing uncertainty, I would encourage you to read my latest book *Risky Business: How Successful Organisations Embrace Uncertainty.*

Cheers
Bryan

# RISK APPETITE

# Embedding Accountability

17 May 2022

I've been speaking to a range of people recently about how to drive accountability for risk management across organisations. More on this coming – watch this space. Interestingly however is sometimes creating accountability starts bottom up and not top down.

One of the reasons I get asked to help with risk appetite statements is because middle management are asking for clarity on the board and executive's appetite for risk in certain areas of the business. They are unsure. Senior leadership needs to respond which leads to creation of a RAS and, if done well and operationalised, leads to a whole new level of accountability at the top and throughout the organisation. Here is an example.

Last year I had a birthday bash to celebrate 20 years of my consulting practice. I invited a few past clients to be interviewed to put a light on some of the lessons I have learnt about risk management over the years. My greatest thanks to each of them for their willingness to share their story.

One of my clients was Val King. We spoke about risk appetite and the work we did together when she was at a water utility a few years ago. The first part of our conversation was about the why and the what of risk

risk appetite statement means faster and better decision making. It provides more decision makers with more clarity about the boundaries within which they can safely operate.

Like much guidance to staff, how the guidance on risk appetite manifests in day-to-day decision making does not happen by simply publishing the guidance. It needs to be operationalised, that is, embedded into the DNA of the organisation.

For more on risk appetite, here is Chapter 8 from my book *Risky Business: How Successful Organisations Embrace Uncertainty* .

Next week's blog will be on operationalising your risk appetite statement.

Cheers
Bryan

*Operationalisation
is the process
of translating
the board and
executive's appetite
for doing business.*

# Operationalising the "A" Word
21 June 2022

Appetite is the "A" word. For many it is a vexed issue (see last week's blog 'Implied versus Complied' on the benefits of a Risk Appetite Statement).

Operationalisation is the process of translating the board and executive's appetite for doing business. As is the preference of some, it will be through financial delegations and rates of return on investments, as examples. While many things can be expressed in financial terms, not all can. Even though a project might meet a hurdle rate, it doesn't mean the whole concept turns your customers away from you, resulting in financial loss that was never contemplated in appetite for risk discussion.

First you need to ensure your risk appetite is expressed based on the risk you are willing to take to achieve your objectives (I've said this for more than a decade and here is a COSO paper from 2020 saying the same). Saying you have a low appetite for reputation risk is not helpful. Who doesn't want to protect their reputation with those they care about?

Assuming you have the right approach to your appetite statement, your first step for operationalising it is to ensure the organisation's policies, frameworks, processes and systems are aligned. That is, the guidance they provide to staff will help them make decisions within appetite for risk and will guide them to escalate decisions when not. Yes, that includes financial delegations, investment criteria and a host of other finance related artefacts. It also includes everything from recruitment frameworks and performance reviews to stakeholder consultation and external communication frameworks, if you have them. The aim is to allow decisions to be made quickly when within appetite, by providing staff with guidance from where they currently seek guidance. It is NOT about expansion of the risk framework!

Next week is stage two of operationalising your appetite for business.

Cheers
Bryan

# Appetite on the Rocks
28 June 2022

You have an appetite statement that is expressed on my blog last week 'Operationalising the "A" word' in terms of the risk you are willing to take to achieve your objectives and you have started operationalising it via your policies, frameworks, processes and systems. Next is training.

Who is going to review all of your key policies, frameworks, processes and systems to ensure they align with the risk appetite statement and provide good guidance to help staff make good risk-based decisions within appetite for risk? You? Big job, even if you had the authority to modify them. The answer is: the people working for the executive and the staff who work for them. Which means, they are going to need to have more than a good understanding of the statement.

When I am asked to train management in the organisation's appetite for risk I always use a "life saver flags on the beach" analogy. Here in Australia we have a prominent beach culture and so everyone gets it. I explain that the job of the board and executive is to articulate as best they can, where the flags should be placed on the beach – which indicate where it is "safe to play". That is, it is safe to make decisions within them. If you are too far towards the rocks, you are taking more risk than they want and you need to get back between the flags. If you are outside the flag towards the other end of the beach, you are being too cautious and you need to take more risk to increase the potential reward for the risks being taken.

In my experience, you can give leaders clarity and inspiration on appetite for risk in 60 to 90 minutes. A sound investment of everyone's time, given that the result is faster decisions made within the appetite for risk.

Next week is stage three of operationalising your appetite for business.

Cheers
Bryan

# Appetite over Lunch

5 July 2022

You have a top-notch risk appetite statement, you have started the process of a review of your policies, frameworks, processes and systems to ensure they are aligned by training leaders, as I wrote on my blog "Appetite on the Rocks". Now what?

When I run training for leaders to understand their organisation's risk appetite statement, I ask them exactly the same thing. We discuss how policies, framework, processes and systems work in guiding decision making. They identify that some guidance is through "hard-wiring" such as a procurement system that does not let a procurement go through without certain criteria being met and with the right level of signoffs. At the other extreme the guidance is much more subjective. For example, a stakeholder consultation framework that provides guidance to staff on the level of consultation. It's difficult to hard wire the quality of the consultations.

How can your leaders help staff to understand appetite for risk when some guidance is subjective? The answer I guide them to is "Lunch and Learns" – or their organisation's version of it. A Lunch and Learn is informal training where staff bring their lunch to the session and the group discuss the learning topic. In this case, the leader will bring a decision (past or upcoming) and facilitate a discussion on how the guidance on appetite for risk might be interpreted.

While the leader can't transfer all of their thinking about appetite for risk in one session, they can impart some critical points and over time grow the team's understanding. Team decision making will improve accordingly.

As my Mum used to say: "Good things don't all come at once!"

Cheers
Bryan

*While the leader can't transfer all of their thinking about appetite for risk in one session, they can impart some critical points and over time grow the team's understanding.*

# Devolve to Evolve

27 September 2022

In their McKinsey article "Decision-making: how leaders can get out of the way", Iskandar Amino, Aaron De Smet and Kanika Kakkar highlight the need to devolve decision making for organisations to become more agile. One thing they did not mention was that devolved decision making needs communication about the organisation's appetite for risk in certain areas of the business. In enterprise risk management terms, that means operationalising a Risk Appetite Statement (RAS).

I have written frequently about the pros and cons of developing a RAS. I recognise how challenging it can be, however, more and more organisations have managed to achieve sensible, helpful statements, supported in many cases with well thought through KRIs. However, more and more I am being called on to help operationalise the RAS.

Over the coming weeks I am going to reflect on what is most important when it comes to operationalising your RAS. I'll give you some tips on what to avoid and what to work hardest on. Before I do, for those of you who still question if a RAS is worth pursuing, let me ask you one question: "Does everyone in your organisation have the same appetite for risk taking?" One of my favourite blogs highlights our varying appetites for risk – Bazza and The

Publican's Appetite for Risk. Thanks again "Mike" for letting me use that photo of your backside 😊

If you would like to read more on risk appetite, <u>here</u> is the chapter on risk appetite from my 2021 book *Risky Business: How Successful Organisations Embrace Uncertainty.*

Cheers
Bryan

# Rolling Out – Craps
4 October 2022

Craps is a gambling game using dice. It became well-known to me from the Hollywood movies of mid last century when players gathered around a Craps table and rolled and cheered or expressed their frustration at loss after loss.

Before you start rolling out your Risk Appetite Statement (RAS), and <u>devolving decision making</u> to evolve your organisation, as I wrote last week, you need to consider the quality of the RAS you have to roll out.

If you have ever seen those Hollywood movies when they play Craps, many times you would have sensed the stress amongst the players who were playing for high stakes. Those with a higher appetite for risk taking. An appetite for higher risk taking is obvious. One of the biggest mistakes I have seen organisations make is to prepare a RAS that is risk averse in many areas where the organisation is obviously, to anyone who works there, anything but. They see the pressure applied to "win", to take short cuts, to overlook due process to get the outcome sought. These types of statements are false, often written with fluffy or flowery words that are just spin.

Have a look at **Figure 4**. A fluffy and false RAS is at the bottom. Rolling that out will damage your culture because staff will smell a rat. More commonly I see convenient, bland statements that are pretty meaningless. They provide little guidance to decision makers other than: "Don't do anything to harm our reputation" while setting unrealistic KPIs and pushing people hard to get them.

| Authenticity | Statement | Culture |
|---|---|---|
| Genuine | Compelling | Strengthens |
| Convenient | Bland | Stagnates |
| False | Fluffy | Damages |

Figure 4: Compelling Risk Appetite Statements

What you need is a genuine statement that is compelling for staff, that will result in the agility I wrote about last week. Better, faster decision making within an agreed appetite for risk. Unfortunately when I work with boards and leadership teams, too often they ask for the genuine and compelling one and fight hard to deliver one of convenience written in bland business risk speak.

First you need to fight hard to get the best RAS you can get, then you can move to rolling out the gold! For tips on how to create a good RAS, here is the chapter on risk appetite from my 2021 book *Risky Business: How Successful Organisations Embrace Uncertainty*. Or check out the <u>COSO paper on Risk Appetite</u> from 2020 which also strongly pushes for genuine statements on the organisation's objectives.

Cheers
Bryan

# Map It
11 October 2022

You have your top-notch RAS as I wrote on my blog 'Devolve to Evolve' and you are ready to devolve decision making by operationalising it, see my blog 'Rolling Out – Craps'. My number one tip for operationalising your RAS comes from reading a book first published in 1946. It is called *Administrative Behaviour, A Study of Decision-Making Processes in Administrative Organisations* by Herbert A. Simon. Simon is a Nobel Prize winner, no less.

To summarise his book in a nutshell. An organisation is formed to fulfill a purpose. People in the organisation make decisions to act or not act in pursuit of that purpose. They are trying to make optimum decisions by considering all future possible consequences from the options available and making their best choice. The upper echelons of organisations develop policies, frameworks, procedures, processes and systems to guide the decision making of staff. That's it. That's an organisation. People make decisions to act or not act in pursuit of a purpose provided with guidance in various forms.

As decision makers are being guided by these various decision influencing tools, these tools become mission critical for you. If they do not reflect the RAS, decisions will be potentially flawed. You will need to work with the owners of all these tools, the policy and framework owners and the designers of processes and systems to ensure they reflect the RAS.

Most organisations have a raft of these tools, therefore you need to prioritise. That means, you need to map your RAS to the key tools that best translate the RAS into reality for staff and then work with the owner to ensure it is fit for purpose. Take procurement for example: if you want value for money with very little risk of fraud or other probity issues, you must ensure the procurement framework delivers this. On the other hand, if you want a more agile organisation you may need to work with the procurement lead to tame the framework.

However, before you approach the key influencing tool owners, you will need to engage with them in the right way. That is the topic for next week's blog.

Have you downloaded yet the chapter on risk appetite from my 2021 book *Risky Business: How Successful Organisations Embrace Uncertainty*?

Cheers
Bryan

# Ding the Bell
18 October 2022

You have heard the term "Tone from the Top". To operationalise your RAS you are going to need to "ding the bell" to make sure the leadership team are delivering the right tone. When I say leadership team, I'm talking the broader leadership team, not the executive that worked with the board to establish the RAS. Hopefully they are onboard.

I used to say that a RAS was between the board and the executive and not to publish it broadly because a RAS is difficult to interpret if you weren't part of the conversation in the first place. Just make sure your policies, processes and systems reflect the RAS, as I wrote on my blog 'Map It'. Yes, some sharing of the RAS with leaders outside the Executive was needed but not en masse.

Over the years, staff in organisations have become more sophisticated when it comes to enterprise risk management. Extended leadership teams needed to both understand the RAS, and wanted to. They wanted to understand it so they could get on with their jobs and lead, rather than take a punt they were doing the right thing or having to refer decisions because they weren't confident to take a punt.

This has meant I have had the opportunity to work with

extended leadership teams in many organisations to help them understand the purpose and importance of a RAS (see my blog 'Devolve to Evolve') and to discuss with them how best to operationalise the RAS. During these sessions I tell them about Herbert Simon's book *Administrative Behaviour* I wrote about last week and impress on them to review their policies and procedures as needs be.

The other tip is for leaders to sit down with their teams to discuss a past decision or a pending decision using the RAS. These statements are so nuanced it takes a conversation such as these to convey the real meaning of the RAS. My tip is to do this not once, but as many times as needed, to be comfortable the RAS is well understood. Even then sometimes team members will need help and that is where decision support tools come in. More on that next week.

Cheers
Bryan

# Go Mental
25 October 2022

If you are going to fully operationalise your Risk Appetite Statement (RAS) you need to go mental. Developing Mental Models is what I am talking about. Let me explain.

Over the past month I have suggested you need to: support your teams by documenting the organisation's appetite for risk (see my blog 'Rolling Out – Craps'); guide their decision making by reviewing and improving policies, frameworks and procedures (see my blog 'Map It') to reflect appetite for risk; work with your teams to discuss how to apply the RAS (see my blog 'Ding the Bell') in decision making.

Now you can get really serious. You see, the way we make decisions are influenced by our own mental models of how a decision is to be made. A mental model is our mental diagram of who and what is involved in a decision, at what point in time it will be made and where the decision is made. For example: a steering committee versus a team meeting. Research has shown that if we leave individuals to create their own mental model, there is a big risk of high variability in decision making, and that when a team co-creates a mental model with key stakeholders, the

*If you are going to fully operationalise your Risk Appetite Statement (RAS) you need to go mental. Developing Mental Models is what I am talking about.*

team's performance becomes far more compelling and the team is able to accelerate towards achieving its goals[3].

The approach I take is influenced by my Chemical Engineering background. I prefer agreed symbols and nomenclature and the development of a process map. Others get more artistic using images and paying more attention to style. What's important is whatever works for the team. For a team of engineers – lines and symbols. The marketing department – more creative and artistic please.

Once the process map is built it is useful in two ways. One, look at it and improve it. Remove bottlenecks for example. Two, identify areas for improving the decision through better inputs, better processes for making group decisions and better communication of the decision to those that need to know. Remember, communicating is the hardest thing (see my blog 'What is the hardest thing for a leader to do?') for a leader to do really, really well!

There will be more on improving decision processes next week, but in the meantime, if you want to get deeper into decision mapping check out this link.

Cheers
Bryan

---

3   Jeffery, Arthur B and Maes, Jeanne D and Bratton-Jeffery, Mary F: Improving team decision-making performance with collaborative modelling, Team Performance Management Vol. 11 No. ½, 2005, pp. 40-50.

# JudgeMENTAL
1 November 2022

I love coming up with the cute, pithy, epigrammatic or aphoristic titles for my blogs 😊 I also love a good thesaurus!

Last week I espoused the co-creation of a decision map to improve your team's decisions. That is, to co-create a MENTAL model of how the decision is made and look for ways to improve the decision maker(s) JUDGEMENT.

Improving judgement can be from any number of types of decision support tools. From guidelines to sophisticated data models built using machine learning or AI. The most basic are:

**Rapid Ranking:** A tool designed to score options for a decision to identify which rates the highest from a set of defined criteria. *Example:* To determine if an option is too risky.

**Decision Trees:** A guidance tool that asks for Yes or No answers to flow down – or across the tree to an end point. *Example:* To determine if a breach requires compulsory reporting.

**Multi-Criteria Decision Analysis:** Used to assist a decision maker to play one positive aspect of a decision against a negative aspect. *Example:* To balance impact on the environment with economic benefit decisions.

Each of these can help operationalise your risk appetite statement. First identify where most variability in decision making (when it comes to risk appetite) is occurring and then consider if one of these tools are the answer. If not, then the answer might be in other options I will write about next week.

For more on decision making and why we get decisions wrong, you might want to check out this whitepaper called Think it Through.

Cheers
Bryan

# Go MENTAL Together
8 November 2022

If you have been reading my blogs these past six weeks, you will know what I mean by Go Mental. And that means co-creating a decision map to improve your team's decisions. Last week I introduced some very simple tools, while mentioning more sophisticated tools like data models built using machine learning or AI.

If you design and utilise simple tools like rapid ranking or decision trees, often these are only used as inputs to a decision to be made by a group. And we all know that groupthink is a thing.

Group decisions can be flawed – peer pressure and the loudest voice in the room are two examples. Research has shown that group decision making can be improved by averaging group independent assessments[4]. Other research shows that decisions can be further improved by groups creating a robust average of assessments where extreme outliers are excluded[5].

One option I utilise is anonymous voting. Modern

---

4   Jack L. Treynor (1987) Market Efficiency and the Bean Jar Experiment, Financial Analysts Journal, 43:3, 50-53, DOI: 10.2469/faj.v43.n3.50

5   Mariano Sigman and Dan Ariely (2017) How can groups make good decisions? | TED Studio

apps like Slido and Mentimeter make this relatively straightforward depending on what is being assessed. For example, providing a range of choices across an interval scale where the intervals are proportionate. This does however cause conflict between a practical versus academic, or pure statistical view, as to whether you can average an Ordinal or Likert scale. The practical view is that the averaging is helpful in decision making[6], and 80% of the time I will always go for practical. However, sometimes a decision is so critical, any misguidance from misguided science must be avoided!

For more on decision making and why we get decisions wrong, check out this whitepaper called Think it Through.

Cheers
Bryan

---

6    Jeff Sauro, (2016) Can you take the mean of ordinal data?, MeasuringU

# Suffer the Consequences
15 November 2022

This is the last in my series on operationalising risk appetite and I am coming back into the mainstream with the use of risk criteria and the risk matrix.

I wrote a blog a couple of years ago called "Escaping the Matrix". In it I mentioned there are many, many risk practitioners who are calling for the scrapping of the risk matrix. While the risk matrix has its problems, at least it has given us a decision support tool that facilitates great conversations that need to be had, and it can be used as the starting point of getting accurate with risk analysis.

In my Risk Leadership Group a few weeks ago we had session on risk tolerances and risk criteria. Some of the more practical problems for the development of risk criteria came up. Issues like criteria that indicates a Rare likelihood risk rating is less than once every three years. I would not want the potential for fatality or my organisation being blown apart every four plus years! I want rare to mean rare.

It prompted me to revisit the risk criteria template I use. The problem that was coming up way too often for my clients was insufficient granularity. Too many risks clustered in Medium and High. Not many Lows and, fortunately and understandably, very few Extreme risks. So I adjusted my likelihood criteria to make higher likelihood events higher risk and lower likelihood events lower risk. Essentially shifting appetite for risk.

While this is a simple act, it needs to be done to reflect the appetite for risk of the organisation. If done poorly, you will end up with an organisation seeing your risk criteria as fluffy and false which, as I pointed out in respect to your RAS (see my blog 'Rolling Out – Craps'), can damage your culture. And so to my last words on operationalising risk in this series. The board sets the risk appetite for the organisation. The executive champion it. Management operationalise it. And staff need to "live it".

That's right, it is ALL about culture.

For more on building the right culture in your organisation, check out this whitepaper on developing risk champions.

Cheers
Bryan

# Risk Appetite – Aligning the Poles

20 April 2021

Your staff come to work and bring their best selves (mostly). However, their best selves have a different appetite for risk taking. If you haven't already, survey their attitude to risk to their personal safety or their personal financial risk. Herein lies the need for them to understand the organisation's appetite for risk taking, so that they can make the right decision way more often than not.

There is another often overlooked need for the board and exec's appetite for risk taking to be embedded in the DNA of your organisation. This story I tell in my book *Risky Business: How Successful Organisations Embrace Uncertainty*, explains it:

> *There's one more phenomenon you need to understand, however. It became very clear to me years ago when I was running risk champions training for a team tasked with putting workers in a high-risk and emotionally stressful environment. I was talking about the need to design policies, processes and systems to guide decision making 'so staff will make the same decision the CEO would make'. Then, from the middle of the pack of 25 in*

*the room came, 'Bullshit! The CEO would not know shit when it comes to some of the decisions we need to make.*

And there you have it. Leaders hire staff with specialist skills to get the job done. The CEO can't be a specialist in all areas. So what happens in organisations is that senior management are trying to influence decision making of staff. Meanwhile staff are looking back at the executives in their 'ivory tower' and saying to themselves, *They have no idea!* and they try to influence the executive. And poor middle management is caught in the middle.

It's like what happens when two magnets are brought close to each other when the poles are reversed (Figure 5). The flow of the magnetic field from north to south is interrupted. Getting risk appetite right is the beginning of alignment of the poles, where decisions are made within appetite, or are escalated if they are not, and information is fed back to decision makers to increase the knowledge and overall capability of staff throughout the organisation.

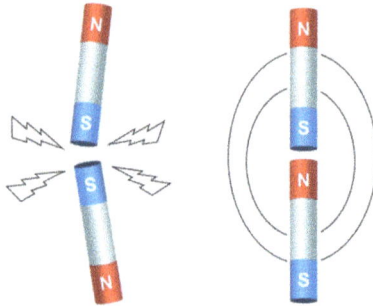

Figure 5: Risk Appetite – Aligning the Poles

I believe risk appetite matters. BUT it is not as easy as saying, "Let's have one."

If you want to know more about my thoughts on risk appetite download my whitepaper or, better still, buy my book and gain access to my latest risk appetite templates.

Stay safe!

Cheers
Bryan

PS I'm thrilled to say my book *Risky Business* hit the #1 Amazon Best Seller list recently in the Risk Management Category. If you have read it and think it's worthy of a review, I would greatly appreciate your time in leaving one. You would make this risk nerd very, very happy. You can email it through to me HERE.

*I believe risk appetite matters. BUT it is not as easy as saying, "Let's have one."*

# Bazza and the Publican's Appetite for Risk

27 April 2021

I love using this example of why you need to agree, and to operationalise, risk appetite for staff – to <u>align the poles</u> so to speak. It is not a corporate example. It is from everyday living. Well not quite every day, but you will get the gist.

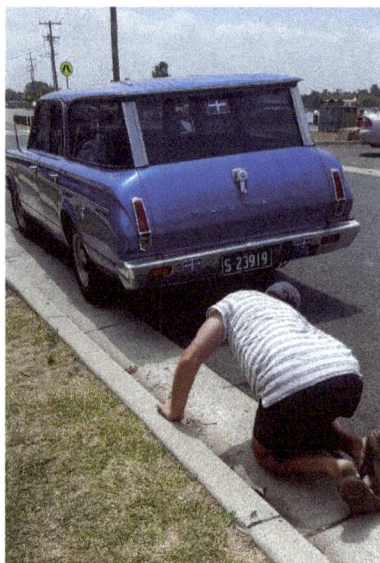

I was "up the coast" one summer. A term well understood for those who live in Sydney as it covers anywhere from the Central Coast to the Queensland border. As with most holidays you get a good story or three. One of mine is the quintessential Aussie story as well as a wonderful depiction of why leaders in organisations need to know staff are operating within the bounds of the leadership team's appetite for business.

My friend (let's call him Mike) and I were walking towards

a pub. A few of us were taking interest in an old Valiant (an Aussie-made car by Chrysler until 1981) outside the pub. Soon Mike and I were looking at a snake poking its head out from under the wheel well on the back left of the car. My friend decided to take a closer look and I was ready with the camera in case I was able to capture a spectacular moment.

(Un)Fortunately nothing happened to my friend and we went inside for a beer. A while later I heard a patron speaking to the publican.

Patron: "Did you hear Frankie from up whoop whoop way came into town with a python wrapped up in his wheel well?"

Publican: "You don't say."

Patron: "Yeh. Bazza grabbed it and has let it out back in the bushes."

Publican: "Where in the bushes?"

Patron: "In the beer garden." (A beer garden is an outside area for food and drinks at an Aussie pub).

Publican: "You can't let a bloody snake loose in the beer garden! It's irresponsible!"

Not long after hearing this interaction, Mike and I had to get moving. I ducked around the corner to a shop while he headed to the car. By the time I met him in the car he was laughing his head off. Apparently, the publican had just walked past with the snake in a pillowcase. My friend explained what had transpired.

The publican had gone and found Bazza, calling him irresponsible along with a few other names. Bazza had then done the right thing (as far as he was concerned) and grabbed the snake and put it in the pillowcase. Presumably, the publican called the wildlife rescue service for the safe relocation of the snake. As they walk past Mike's car he hears:

Patron: "Well I got the snake for you. How about a free beer!"

Publican: "A free beer? No way. You're bloody-well irresponsible!"

The take-away from this story for you is that staff members have personal biases that stem from their VEG (values, environment and genes) (see my blog, VEGetables underlie clear thinking) resulting in different perceptions of risk. Obviously Bazza thought nothing of dealing with a python while the publican knew that people in the beer garden would more than likely freak out if they saw a snake. Even if the snake was relatively harmless (pythons are non-venomous and very rarely attack humans as they swallow their prey whole).

Given we all have different perceptions of risk, as leaders in organisations it is an imperative that staff know your tolerances for risk taking.

If you want to know more about my thoughts on risk appetite download my _whitepaper_ or, better still, buy my book _Risky Business: How Successful Organisations Embrace Uncertainty_ and gain access to my latest risk appetite templates.

Stay safe!

Cheers
Bryan

*I wrote about how your staff come to work and bring their best selves (mostly). However, their best selves have a different appetite for risk taking, and that means inconsistency in decision making. Sometimes, alarming decisions are made.*

# Embedding Appetite into Your DNA

15 June 2021

A couple of months back on my blog 'Risk Appetite – Aligning the Poles', I wrote about how your staff come to work and bring their best selves (mostly). However, their best selves have a different appetite for risk taking, and that means inconsistency in decision making. Sometimes, alarming decisions are made.

Last month I had a birthday bash to celebrate 20 years of my consulting practice. I invited a few past clients to be interviewed to put a light on some of the lessons I have learnt about risk management over the years. My greatest thanks to each of them for their willingness to share their story.

One of my clients was Val King. We spoke about risk appetite and the work we did together when she was at a water utility a few years ago. The first part of our conversation was about the why and the what of risk appetite (check out a clip of our conversation here). The second part was Val explaining the practical implications of embedding appetite into the business.

She spoke about the "a-ha!" moments, when the engineers had tangible guidance that guided their decisions on maintenance schedules and linked the business continuity management framework to decision making on building redundancy into systems. You can check out that part of our chat <u>here</u>.

If you want to know more about my thoughts on risk appetite, download my <u>whitepaper</u> or, better still, buy my <u>book</u> and gain access to my latest risk appetite templates.

Stay safe!

Cheers
Bryan

# The Film Director's Risk Appetite

25 January 2022

A couple of years back I started my year of blogging with a story from my summer holiday time about risk appetite (see my blog 'Bazza and The Publican's Appetite for Risk). As the modern plague (I can't call it the C word thanks to spam filters) took a new twist over my summer, I of course observed the various appetites for risk portrayed across the spectrum that is our diverse society.

In my opinion, no one person or group of people can claim theirs is the right stance to take. Everyone has different circumstances and different perspectives. Take my twenty-year-something kids. Two of three, Doug and Ben, just got on with life as normal. Caught it. Got over it pretty quickly. On they go.

My third child, Emily, was due to shoot a short film for her final project of her university degree. It was set for Monday through Wednesday of last week. She hunkered down and avoided all the hotspots and while all her friends caught it, she managed to avoid it.

Then there was the dozen or so cast and crew she needed to worry about, as she was the Director. Watching her manage the uncertainty was impressive. She had understudies and backup crew all sorted. Test kits arranged. All was set for the venues, which were people's homes. This is where things started to come unstuck. The weather meant shifting one venue to a different day and another one was pulled just a few days before. Apparently, the owners did not really want a dozen magnets of the modern plague to roam their house for a day.

It was at this point that I found out our house was the substitute, and that my wife and I needed to vacate it and take the dog with us! Suffice to say we somehow found a lovely cabin on a lake and had a great couple of days away.

The shoot went ahead without any major hitches, and we are all looking forward to seeing the final product.

It was the week before that Emily said something that epitomised the current state of play for so many. "It's making it fifteen times harder!" Her planning (some may even call it risk management 😀) helped her push through and seize the day. Something we are all going to have to do a lot more of in the coming months.

So with that said ... good luck with your planning, seize the day and please stay safe!

Cheers
Bryan

# RISK ASSESSMENT

# No Regrets
2 November 2021

We are all prone to impulsiveness at different times. Sometimes that can lead to one hell of a fun ride and other times it can lead to regret.

For a no regrets lifestyle we need to work with our tendency for impulsiveness. In Daniel Kahnemann's book *Thinking Fast and Slow* he gives more than forty heuristics, where we take mental shortcuts to make a quicker decision. (Erik Johnson has a nice summary of each of them here). Kahnemann explains how each of these are by no means foolproof and suggests that we need to identify the times when we should slow down our thinking to check if the heuristic in play is valid in each case.

Risk assessment is one form of thinking slow. Taking the time to deliberate possible outcomes and their likelihood of occurrence. However, not everything needs a risk assessment. Hence, I came up with my own decision model that can be applied rapidly to any decision. I call it the MCI Decision Model.

My model checks if you have gone straight to **Implementation** mode without the Clarification that comes from developing and comparing a suite of options and confirms if your Motivation behind your decision is creating positive or negative blockers to your decision making.

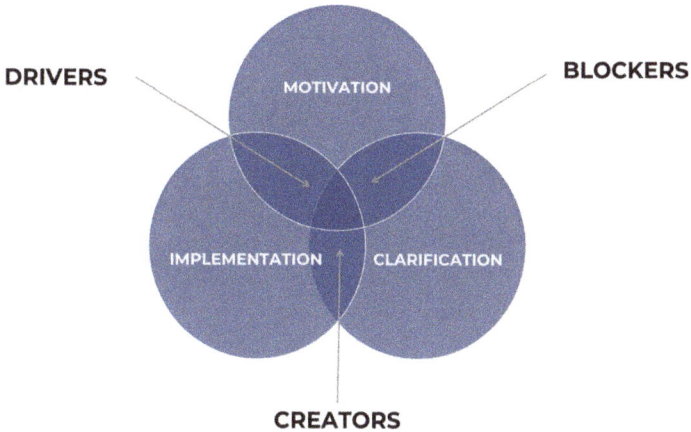

Figure 6: MCI Decision Model

Whether you are fussing over a decision as to where to eat tonight, or a bigger decision, my MCI Decision Model will quickly test your thinking.

You can read more about it in this paper – _Think it Through._

Cheers
Bryan

# There Are Only Three Questions
### 30 May 2023

Pretty soon I am publishing a book of my blogs of the last three years and one of my team (my wife Jacquie) pointed out that out of all the blogs, only one of them focuses on risk assessment. A bit bizarre when you think about it, given that this is where the rubber hits the road for the risk management process. It's where a heap of value from your risk framework is delivered.

Funnily enough, there are only three questions you need to ask in a risk assessment. The first one is obvious: "What could go wrong?" The second one is equally, if not more crucial: "What must go right?" And lastly, the third question: "What are we currently doing about all of this?" While I have been doing this with clients for more than 20 years, I had not encountered such a concise expression of these questions until I heard it expressed so simply from an Australian Tax Office attendee, at the RMIA ERM Course which I run, who explained how simple they make it for their staff. And you probably know I preach simplicity when it comes to risk. Making things too complex has been the biggest failing of the risk profession and an earlier version of me is guilty of it.

I'm sure you get the essence of "What could go wrong?" and "What are we currently doing about all of this?"

*If you are not asking
"What must go right?"
you are missing out
on one key aspect
of the principles of
risk management,
and that is, to
create value and
not just protect it.*

(current controls). However, you might be pondering a little about the second question "What must go right?"

In virtually every strategic plan I come across from various clients, there are strategic initiatives outlined to achieve strategic objectives. This is what I am talking about. This is what I am talking about. What are they and what measures are in play to ensure these initiatives are delivered. These questions posed to an executive team often stir a bit of discomfort, especially after the current controls are rated, as well as the risk level of failing on an initiative. This same principle also applies to projects, change initiatives and a multitude of other business activities.

If you are not asking "What must go right?" you are missing out on one key aspect of the principles of risk management, and that is, to *create* value and not just protect it.

Cheers
Bryan

# MASTERING RISK
# WORKSHOP FACILITATION

# The Big Thrill

22 March 2022

The biggest thrill I get in my role guiding organisations to develop stronger and stronger approaches to risk-based decision making is when I run a risk workshop. In particular, for an executive team or board. In those moments they place their trust in me. Trusting that what they say will never be repeated by me, that the time will be valuably spent, that improved understanding – as opposed to increased confusion – will be the result.

My aim is always to have the Chair, CEO or team leader say to me at the end of the workshop something like this:

> "Thank you. We've never had a conversation quite like that before."

Why is it that it needs to come to this? Why is it that they have not demanded such a conversation in the past?

One reason is they already have robust conversations. That is, they discuss risks to the business all the time. They discuss the pros and cons of their decisions. They are practicing a form of risk management day-in day-out. What more should they do?

Yet we ask more time of them. And they are busy. Very busy. Why should they stop and think more than normal?

Just because a risk professional says: "We should do a risk workshop"?

The answer is because a well-run risk workshop makes them think differently. Because *we* think differently. Let me explain.

A few years back I had a coffee with a senior risk professional from a very large organisation in a high-risk industry. He started the meeting quite flabbergasted. He told me he had just come from a two-hour workshop with a bunch of engineers. They had been discussing one of the organisation-ending enterprise risks that had been identified. The engineers were explaining the controls they had in place. After two hours he explained to them why the controls would not work and excused himself to go to his next meeting (with me where he needed to vent).

It made me reflect that our backgrounds and training mean we often think differently to other people in business. The challenge is to catch their attention, get them thinking without them feeling like we are being negative or critical and then to open their eyes to the possibilities you can see. The POSITIVE as well as the NEGATIVE.

Stay safe and please run engaging workshops.

Cheers
Bryan

*Risk management is about helping others be successful. Identify your target audience's definition of success and explain how the risk workshop will help deliver that. It is not always easy, but you must find a hook.*

it about risk workshops that achieves this? I'll give you to next week to answer the question then I will give you mine. 😌

Stay safe and please run engaging workshops.

Cheers
Bryan

# Sensemaking
5 April 2022

Sensemaking. This is the answer to my question last week about why risk workshops should deliver the success your audience craves. Yes, they identify risks to help us understand the uncertainty surrounding the objectives we wish to achieve. However, in doing so, we are helping the business make sense of a crazy world.

We should not be extracting information from a reluctant team, nor should we be collecting risks to report to the Audit and Risk Committee to get a pat on the back as a job well done. We should, no MUST, be helping the team to make sense of their world so they can make better and better decisions. We must provide insights to challenge them, to open their eyes.

My favourite insight tools are:

- Stakeholder Analysis to identify key opportunities or vulnerabilities associated with key stakeholders that have not previously been identified by the management team. Sample.
- PESTLE Analysis to conduct or update the organisation's previous environmental scans to help establish current and emerging challenges for the organisation. Sample.
- My Capability Analysis which is a method for

assessing internal performance capability by identifying strengths and weaknesses across the five key building blocks of an organisation – Strategy, People, Processes, Assets and Culture. <u>Sample.</u>

If you use these types of tools to provide insights and open eyes, you will provide more value than ever before. You will have a seat at the table as a highly respected facilitator of critical conversations that help ensure the future success of your organisation.

Who would not want that?

Stay safe and please run engaging workshops.

Cheers
Bryan

# Making Sense
12 April 2022

Over the last few weeks, I have encouraged you to look at risk workshops as pathways to creating clarity for teams about what is between them and success. Sensemaking or making sense of the world.

The secret to successful risk workshops is the preparation you undertake. I know you are busy and preparing takes time. However, if there is one tip I give that I wish you would take and always follow, it's to over-prepare for a risk workshop. The more you prepare the more insights you can create for the team, the greater their ability to make sense of their world and the more you are valued.

I remember running a risk workshop about 15 years ago that did not go so well. It is the last time I broke my golden rules about preparing a strong piece of analysis, and making sure I met the two most important people in the room before the day. In this case it was a board, and the two most important people were the Chair and the most vocal or influential board member. All had gone very well with the division workshops I ran and because "everyone is so busy" they did not think I needed to meet them beforehand.

It became a bit of a slanging match between board and exec. When the workshop finished my client commented:

"That did not go too bad." Turns out it was an adversarial relationship between board and management. I would have sensed that had I met with them beforehand and I would have taken a different approach. I would have done more asking for their thoughts, rather than informing them of what management thought were the key risks to the organisation's objectives.

Stay safe and please run engaging workshops.

Cheers
Bryan

# Don't Vacillate

19 April 2022

The more prepared you are the better you will facilitate. The less likely you will vacillate at a difficult moment.

Regardless, the ability to effectively facilitate a workshop is a wonderful skill to develop. When I facilitate, I concentrate on three things:

- To be in service of those in the room. I'm not the star.
- To stimulate critical and creative thinking. I need to unlock their minds.
- To be an advocate for everyone in the room. I will protect and promote.

In doing so you will encounter tense moments. Consequently, you need to develop your ability to be in the moment while at the same time hovering above the room observing everything that is happening.

I think some of the young gamers of today may well be great facilitators. Games where they are working in teams with a helicopter view to one side while the gamer is in the main action. They need to keep one eye on the action, one eye on the big picture and all the while working with their teammates, communicating with them, acting quickly and decisively.

If you can channel your gamer self or learn from a gamer to perfect this art, you will run more effective workshops. No bickering, with plenty of sound discussions and decisive action will be your reward.

Stay safe and please run engaging workshops.

Cheers
Bryan

# Do Validate
26 April 2022

The workshop is over. The hard work is done. The Chair, CEO or team leader has taken you aside and thanked you for such an enlightening workshop. Job done!

No, it's not.

The last thing you need to do is make sure you are helping the team with sensemaking, not nonsense making. The key is a reality-check with the team post the workshop. Not straight after, at least a day, if not a week. Let memories wane a little and then revisit the outcomes and ask a few questions:

- Does this align to our values? Does it pass the pub test?

  How many times have we heard of a decision by a political leader that turns into political suicide? They simply forgot to apply the pub test or they got it horribly wrong.

- Is there data to support the decisions made? Or are we suffering from what I call Quantifornication?

  I am still horrified at the lack of data collection and analysis when it comes to the analysis of risk. Even when data is available, some are much more comfortable going with their gut than with the evidence. The problem is, the gut only has a high degree of accuracy for decisions we have made thousands and thousands of times before. This does not work for business decisions which may only count into the hundreds at best, with others being complete one-offs.

- Is this achievable? Or have we promised more than we can deliver or, simply said, we've committed to things we know won't get done? Are the politics all wrong and will initiatives be blocked as soon as initiated?

  I've seen it so many times. Leaders in risk workshops getting motivated by the discussions only to realise later that their current commitments and budget simply won't allow them to implement what was just agreed to. In this case the answer is to use risk to re-prioritise resources. Managers understand that the highest risk areas should get the resources required.

There you go. The last three blogs have encouraged you to Prepare – Facilitate – Validate. If you want to go deep on this approach, please come to my next training program on <u>Mastering Risk Workshop Facilitation</u>.

Stay safe and please run engaging workshops.

Cheers
Bryan

# A Whitepaper for You on Facilitating Critical Conversations

3 May 2022

If you're an avid reader of my blog you would have noticed over the last six weeks that I've been writing about the importance and skill of facilitating valuable risk workshops. I've also had the pleasure recently of hosting a couple of free MasterClasses on this topic with great success and engagement from my followers.

The message is clear: Becoming a gun facilitator is imperative in making sustainable impact for your colleagues and your organisation.

With many people reaching out to me asking for a recording of my MasterClasses, I've decided to take what's already been written, expand on it further and produce a whitepaper titled _**Risk Workshop Facilitation: the Art and Science of Facilitating Critical Conversations**_.

My hope is that you'll derive great value from my experience over the years of facilitating many, many risk conversations. I've often said it's one of my favourite things to do.

As always, let me know what you think. And remember

*The message is clear: Becoming a gun facilitator is imperative in making sustainable impact for your colleagues and your organisation.*

your goal: To be known as the facilitator of invaluable conversations. If you nail that, you nail your career as a risk professional.

Cheers
Bryan

P.S. For those of you who want to deep dive into training on becoming a gun facilitator, check out my next online Mastering Risk Workshop Facilitation Course. More details and registering option can be found HERE.

# Inconvenient Truths

10 May 2022

Recently I had one of those tickly moments in a risk workshop I was facilitating. I heard the words: "We can't put that up!"

The risk was being assessed inconveniently high. As I have written and spoken about many times before, one of our jobs as risk professionals is to uncover the elephant in the room, if there is one.

Rating risk in the absence of data is highly subjective, and of course true quantification would be preferred. Even so, one can ask questions that reveal some basic data, like: "How many times has it happened in the past?" Memories are searched, incidents remembered, and the inconvenient truth appears.

Then the rationalisation starts. OK, so the likelihood is higher than we thought but the consequences aren't as bad as we first thought. Truthfully, this often proves the case. People have overreacted to the impact because it seems like a big deal. Again a few questions provide data, like the obvious one: "What happened as a result of those incidents?" or: "Did anyone lose their job over it?" "Did the media pick it up?" "How long did the media interest last?"

If the truth is still inconvenient, it's time to look at the risk criteria. Is the definition of Major really that bad?

If you have done all of the above, the inconvenient truth needs to stand. **BUT** how you communicate the risk is critical. A couple of tips:

- Always start with the positives, if any.
- Provide answers in the form of what could be done to manage the situation.
- Point out that this may mean we need to discuss our appetite for risk in this domain, rather than expending resources on what could be done.

Stay safe.

Cheers
Bryan

# Breakthroughs

22 November 2022

Breakthroughs are what you can expect from a good risk workshop.

While I was writing this blog, I had to stop and go into an MS Teams meeting to meet the Chair of the Board of an organisation for whom I had been engaged to run a Board Risk Workshop. I explained the process I was going to use and stated the aim was to ensure a really valuable conversation.

I then asked the Chair if they had any specific expectations. They said, "Sounds excellent. I am always looking for "breakthroughs" from these workshops. That is, by discussing the things that might break us, we find things that allow us to breakthrough."

What timing, I had just sat down to write about "Finding Opportunity through Enterprise Risk Workshops" and was gifted this gold. What the Chair said was absolutely spot on. By improving our understanding of key risks, and the scale of them, we can move onto the question of "What are we going to do about all of that?" And that is when those present step into innovative thinking mode. And the bigger the risk the more innovative the thinking becomes, through necessity. That is, when whatever we have been doing is not good enough, we must try something else or we will simply have to live with it.

Do you have the same experience when you facilitate risk workshops? If not, you might want to look into the process you follow. Hint: it's all in the preparation. Great preparation means great insights for decision makers. Something I go to in great detail in my Mastering Risk Workshop Facilitation Course.

Cheers
Bryan

# Undersexed

29 November 2022

A couple of weeks ago I ran a MasterClass on "How to run an impactful risk workshop". One of the questions asked at the end of the session was:

> "Coming from an organisation that's been running an Enterprise Risk Framework for many years and successfully lifting Risk Maturity, there are subtle hints of risk management fatigue. Would love some tips on how we can keep things lively!"

On the one hand I would like to question how mature the organisation's risk culture is if there are signs of fatigue. In the most mature organisations, the management of risk is a leadership imperative. Not done for the comfort of the board or regulator. It is simply how we do business.

Having said that, I get that updating risk profiles in the absence of major organisational change can be less than awe inspiring. What is needed is for things to be sexed up a bit. My top three tips would be:

1. Focus on what has changed in the business and the potential change in risk profile.
2. Introduce new analysis tools. As a minimum I use stakeholder, PESTLE and my Capability Analysis tools (available from my website). So

besides updating them I would think about introducing Industry Five Forces or Unique Selling Proposition or maybe some Value Chain analysis.

3. Infographics. Google infographic "topic of risk assessment" (e.g. infographic payroll) and see if there is a graphic you can use as is or one that gives you some ideas as to how you can represent some of the data associated with the topic.

BTW, it doesn't hurt to have a bit of fun in risk workshops. I often will run a fun activity that makes a point about the value of risk assessment. See this TikTok video by Simon Sinek for the importance of enjoyment at work.

Come to my Mastering Risk Workshop Facilitation Course and you will experience one of my fun activities!

Cheers
Bryan

# Buying Time
6 December 2022

In my blog last week I answered a question which came up during my MasterClass on "How to run an impactful risk workshop", about tackling risk management fatigue (see my blog 'Undersexed'). Another question was asked during the workshop concerning that finite resource, time:

> "Do you typically run multiple workshops for the one business unit? E.g. A risk identification workshop first and then another to explore the detail? How do you overcome time constraints? I find that people often get bogged down on exploring the first couple of risks and we run out of time."

My answer is that I buy time. That is, I ask for the maximum time I can get for a workshop, take what I get, give the participants a valuable experience and I have subsequently bought more time. That is, they want to, or are at least willing to, have another session because they know there was important unfinished business.

I usually can get two hours with a board or executive team. Much can be accomplished in that time but there is still plenty of work to do afterwards to get final agreement on the risk profile and all the actions that need to be taken. Occasionally I get three or four hours but there is still work to be done afterwards because there are always things that need to be followed up with others. So I don't try and land the whole profile in that time. I prefer to take the extra time to explore potential areas of risk and to have richer conversations about the ones identified.

I recommend against workshops exceeding half a day. Too many participants either cancel last moment or duck out too often. Instead, I buy time.

Cheers
Bryan

# Criss Cross

13 December 2022

Another question from my MasterClass on "How to run an impactful risk workshop" was:

> "Have you used or encountered use of a cross-sectional risk methodology e.g. run finance/budget related risk workshops for a department and invite a Finance SME to facilitate?"

My answer: "No I haven't but what a great idea!"

What I do recommend is that you have internal stakeholders attend whenever you run a risk workshop. They could be customers of yours or they may be suppliers. They learn more about your business challenges and become more understanding as a minimum. More likely they give independent views and ask interesting questions that make the team think differently. I find them highly valuable participants.

The other benefit to you is that they change. Internal suppliers provide you a better service and internal customers work more cooperatively with you.

If you have an SME facilitate a risk workshop (well) for a team, I'm sure that workshop would rock. It's another way to spice things up – a topic I dealt with a couple of weeks ago.

*Criss Crossing is also an antidote to the effect of silos in organisations. They break them down by ensuring communication is improved between them.*

Criss Crossing is also an antidote to the effect of silos in organisations. They break them down by ensuring communication is improved between them. Which leads me to one more question asked in the MasterClass on risk workshops:

> "What are the main indicators of business unit silos and how do we begin to overcome them?"

My answer: "There are no indicators. They simply exist. We put people into business units which mean we put people into silos. They must be dealt with."

Hence the need to Criss Cross!

Cheers
Bryan

# Painting Murals

31 August 2021

I have long been speaking about painting pictures (see my blog 'Paint Draw Pick to Implement Enterprise Risk Management') to influence others. One of the great things that has come out of the pandemic has been the successful shift to online learning and online facilitating that so many of us have made. In the online environment painting pictures is quicker, easier and can be more compelling than using butcher's paper, post-it notes and a whiteboard.

The tools I use when facilitating online include my Surface Studio with touch screen and pen, the Microsoft whiteboard and my most powerful tool, Mural. From what I can tell, Mural and Miro are the two most popular online collaboration tools.

I now use Mural as a workbook for a training program. I set up a series of "sub-murals" on a mural board and unveil them with content and activities as the session unfolds. Participants are able to drop e-post-it-notes onto the board to make comments or record findings. They can build things like process maps. They can draw and create a story. All of it flows pretty seamlessly, even for those using the tool for the first time.

I am raising this because being in lockdown as many in

Australia are, or being unable to bring teams together across state borders for in-person sessions, is a perfect time to take advantage of these tools. Just like I said when writing about <u>Adaptive Leadership</u> last year, experimentation is critical at this time.

If you want to get a sample of how I use these tools, come to one of my free webinars some time or join one of my variety of <u>training programs</u> coming up. It would be great to see you there!

Stay safe!

Cheers
Bryan

# A New Take on Sailing
26 October 2021

Thankfully, when the world went online due to COVID, I was in front of the curve having already run online workshops for some clients. However for obvious reasons the demand for running risk workshops online has increased and I have been upping my game every step of the way to help guarantee workshop participants get as good, if not a better, experience than in-person.

One of the tools I use is Mural. Last week, in search of something new, I came across their "Sailboat Retrospective". It was originally designed for scrum teams. It gave me a new analogy to use to get new perspectives from participants in risk workshops. Alongside is my "Sailboat Perspective" Mural. You will see I have taken my three key questions for a risk workshop:

1. What must go right?
2. What could go wrong?
3. What are we doing about all that?

... and asked them in a range of different ways.

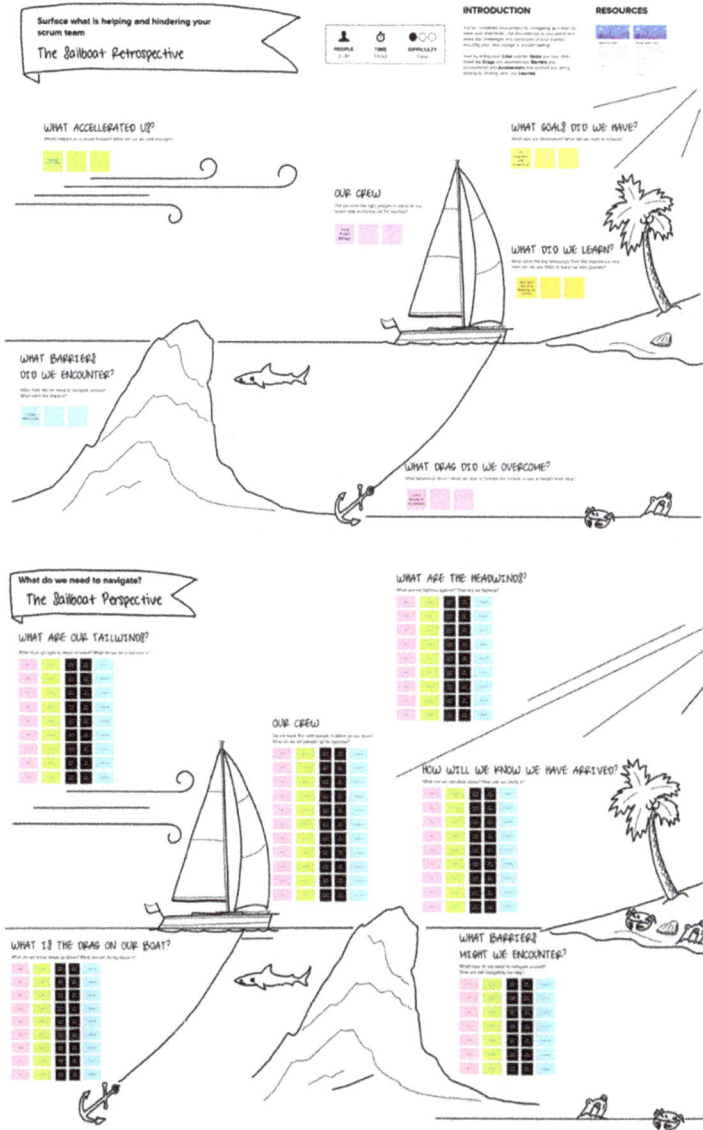

Figure 7: Original and Modified Mural Sailboat Retrospective

Source: Mural

For example, I took the first question about what must go right and created the following alternate questions:

- What are our tailwinds? The ones we depend on to get us where we need to be.
- What is the drag on our boat? The things we know are slowing us down.
- How will we know we have arrived?
- Do we have clarity of goals?
- Can we measure success?

All without using the word "risk".

The result? I usually get great compliments from the likes of CEOs and senior leaders from my risk workshops. Comments like: "That was great. We've never had a conversation like that before." However, this time I reckon I got one better. From the CEO: "Great workshop. It was illuminating!"

Can't help but wonder if we would have had the same or better an outcome if we were in-person?

Cheers
Bryan

# We All Need Insights
## 25 February 2020

Marie Curie provided insight, literally, that anyone would envy.

Ask yourself what *insight* a doctor in World War I would have valued most. Insight, not a wonder drug that is penicillin that was only discovered in the next decade.

Your answer (which I get very quickly when I ask it in workshop) may be "the ability to see bullets". That is, bullets stuck inside the poor souls that had become casualties during the war. Curie designed, built and deployed (with the help of her 17-yr-old daughter) small, portable x-ray machines called Petit Curie. She gave doctors the ability to see bullets and shrapnel lodged in the body as well as bone fractures. Now *that* is insight.

I have the privilege of running workshops for boards, executives, project teams and, funnily enough, marketing insights teams, and every one of them are looking for me to provide them with insights.

When you work with your stakeholders, do you provide them with insights?

I'll give you a tip. If they are looking at their smartphones, rolling their eyes when they come to meetings (ouch), postponing meetings, not showing up to meetings (ouch), they are not getting insights from you.

I don't mean to be harsh. I know you have so much to offer. But so many of our stakeholders are so frigging busy your message does not cut through.

Out of interest. Has my message about industry disruption in my last <u>EIGHT blogs</u> cut through? If so, I want to hear what has resonated. I want your questions. <u>Send them through.</u>

Cheers
Bryan

# RISK CHAMPIONS

# Excited Change Agents
15 March 2022

Every change management challenge needs to be aware of, and harness, change agents. Those people that can most influence or implement the changes required. In the risk space they are often referred to as risk champions.

I wrote an article on <u>risk champions</u> more than ten years ago addressing questions about what you should expect from them and how you should equip them. In it I spoke about how you might lead this group. Let's go one step further and ask how you might excite them into more and more effective change.

The answer, as many things do, comes in a set of three. You need to collaborate with them, challenge them and, with their help, you need to create the interface that links risk management with business decision making.

The power of a challenge, the enjoyment of collaborating and the reward of creating something tangible and useful will excite them. Trust me. I've seen it time and time again. People like to help and be part of a team that makes a difference.

As importantly, this act of co-creation ensures a common understanding of how the interface between risk and the business works, its importance and what can be done to ensure it works effectively, so that risk-based decision making becomes business-as-usual. Then you and they and the business are all on a winner.

For a further read on <u>Risk Champions</u> click here or click this section of my <u>website</u>.

Stay safe and make change.

Cheers
Bryan

# Experts Need Advocates
6 June 2023

No one doubts your expertise. Staff know when they need to come to you. They know they won't get their budget approved without engaging with finance, recruit without HR, get the final approval without compliance and on the list goes. The problem is their perception of what you do. Here is a list I would love to add to if you have a good one and time to reply:

- Finance – Bean Counters
- Compliance – BPOs (Business Prevention Officers)
- IT – Nerds
- Marketing – Colour-in-erors
- Environment – Tree Huggers
- Risk – Fun Police
- HR – People Huggers

## Pigeonholed

It is natural for humans to pigeonhole things. We have a lot on our minds and the amount of information we need to process is increasingly overwhelming so our need to pigeonhole will only increase. It is easier for the business to think of support functions in simple terms than in the more complex, value-adding support you can provide.

## Your Predecessors are Part of the Problem

One of the problems is that not all in your profession has made the profession proud. Too many have been fixated on best practice rather than doing the job well enough to allow the business to perform. Knowing what is well enough is the key. Knowing when to hold or give ground.

## Understand the Business Very, Very Well

In order to know when to give ground you need to truly understand the business you serve. Most people in support functions don't come from the business that they serve as they trained in their profession. So it is difficult to know the business as well as you would like.

There are ways to learn the business. Immersing yourself in it for a period or asking lots and lots of questions and studying the business are all good examples. Even so, you are not in the business and you will not have fully up to date information about them.

## Experts Need Advocates

Enter the advocate. What every support function needs is an advocate in each of the business units you serve. An advocate understands the importance to the business of what you do and they make sure you are given *the time and the information required to add the value you know you can.*

If you don't have a seat at the table, or if you are a last-minute thought, your advocates in the business are not sufficiently influential.  I have written a paper, **<u>Experts Need Advocates</u>** that explores the need for advocates in the business and how you can go about building a tribe to preach your mantra. Feel free to share it with others if you wish.

Cheers
Bryan

# CORPORATE
# COMMUNICATION

# Thodey Nailed It

3 August 2021

I have shared this story before and I just have to share it again as I told it no fewer than six times this week in various presentations and training programs. It is the story of David Thodey, when still CEO of Telstra. He was be interviewed at a UNSW Business School seminar by Narelle Hooper, then Editor of AFR BOSS. Hooper asked a question along these lines: "What is the greatest challenge in running an organisation the size of Telstra?" (which then had over 45,000 employees). Thodey answered (in my words):

> *Getting information I need to know about, from the extremities of the organisation to me, past all the information people are trying to tell me about that I don't need to know, in time for me to do something about it!*

I tell my audience this is what a great enterprise risk management approach to business delivers. It ensures both good and not so good news, gets to those who need to know, to make the best decisions possible. To his credit, Thodey split risk from audit at Telstra and beefed up the team to help the business make better decisions. He doubled the value of Telstra in his time there, however, I'll leave others to pontificate as to his legacy from his time as CEO.

The takeaway from this is, in designing your risk framework, you MUST ensure performance and risk reporting are fully integrated. Otherwise, good news flows quickly, bad news flows poorly, is "massaged" along the way or is suppressed.

You can read more on this in Chapter 5: The End Game from my book *Risky Business: How Successful Organisations Embrace Uncertainty.*

Stay safe!

Cheers
Bryan

# Information Superhighways
## 10 August 2021

How does information we need for decision making flow through the human body to the brain?

The brain gets information from 'the extremities of our organisation' (our body) via our five senses: hearing, sight, touch, smell and taste.

And how is this information channelled through the body?

Via the central nervous system.

Where is the main information superhighway for the central nervous system?

The spine.

How much do we value our spines as human beings?

A lot!

And how much do organisations value their "spine", the information superhighway of the organisation?

Well David Thodey of Telstra valued the spine a lot (see my blog, 'Thodey Nailed It'). However, in my experience many organisations do not. And that is why

# Role Play

23 November 2021

It's interesting how so many things scale in unison. In large organisations there is often talk about silos. But silos exist in small organisations as well. Even for my organisation of three. Me, my EA, Paula and my Relationship Manger, Wendy.

And as you and I know, enterprise risk management is a great tool for breaking down silos. Helping the left hand to know what the right hand is doing through well designed, integrated performance and risk reporting.

And so last week we did some enterprise risk management on our small practice. We looked at the roles each of us play and redefined the silos we operate in.

You see, silos are great for getting stuff done. They allow us to focus on the objectives of our silo and to be clear on what is in and out of the silo. However, when focusing on our silo we tend to ignore what is happening in the other silos.

After re-defining the roles we each play we then thought about our communication needs. What information needs to flow between the three of us. And therein lies one of the biggest challenges in any organisation, getting the right amount of communication, of the right content, delivered in a way that is as easily digestible and actionable as possible.

Anyone involved in the design of your risk framework should think hard about this challenge. Because getting communication right is the hardest thing to do in life. Period.

Stay safe!

Cheers
Bryan

INFLUENCE

# Selling Ice to Inuits
7 September 2021

My Mum used to say "They could sell ice to Eskimos". If you are not familiar with this old saying, it was used to explain that the person can sell something very hard to sell.

Selling risk management is a bit like selling ice to Inuits who obviously would believe they have all the ice they need. Many people think they are terrific at managing risk as evidenced by their success to date. Of course, the world is full of stories of once highly successful people becoming enchanted with their own reputation and making a really bad call. You and I know that unless people stop and think about the uncertainties around a decision and assess those uncertainties based on how likely they are to occur, and the impact they might have, they are not doing risk management.

I am often called on to provide training to senior leaders on risk management and, in particular, risk appetite. Knowing I will have some Inuits in the group means I need to be very, very convincing. I need to be so good people say about me: "He could sell ice to Inuits!"

When it comes to selling the need for an understanding of risk appetite to leaders I start with an online poll. I ask them about their personal appetite for risk about a range of activities. Lo and behold the results show a huge variation in appetite for across the group.

My point? Staff bring their own personal appetite for risk to work and, in the absence of good guidance from the organisation, will apply that in their day-to-day decision making.

Having made my point, I usually double down with a few more reasons why risk appetite should be well understood by them and their teams.

Over the years I have become pretty good at selling the risk management message and, perhaps with a boost from a couple of royal commissions and a pandemic, I am seeing real traction in many, many organisations. If your organisation is not one of them, you best act now. There has never been a better time to get the message across.

Stay safe!

Cheers
Bryan

PS. And if you really want to hone your craft in improving your ability to persuade, join me at my next Persuasive Adviser Program.

# Fighting Your Way Inside the Tent
16 November 2021

Have you ever thought about why internal advisors such as accountants, lawyers, risk managers, auditors, HR managers, IT managers and many other back-of-house advisors struggle to ensure their advice is heeded by the business leaders they are advising? One very big reason is because they are operating "outside the tent". That is, you are not in the same team as those you advise even if you all work for the same organisation. And if you are outside the tent, you lack one of the key elements required to develop trust in a relationship. Teamwork.

If you are an internal advisor, you have probably thought about ensuring your expertise is up to date, that your advice is sound, if not sage-like, and that you deliver it as clearly as possible, so it is understood and acted on. You would have been seeking to develop trust also.

A major problem that is encountered is that internal advisors are tasked with much more than providing this advice and these other tasks can interfere with the relationship and the level of trust. Finance needs to put into place financial controls for example, usually along with a bunch of other administrative controls such as for travel and procurement. HR and IT do the same, as does legal and as do risk and compliance people ... while auditors are often seen as good cop and bad cop all in one. These controls create friction between the support departments and management. This leads to complaints and/or excuses being wielded in various cross-department forums.

The challenge of course is striking a balance. No one likes a back-office tyrant. However, how many of the advisors in your organisation that provide you advice, or that work for you, gets the balance right? How many are cutting through with their advice and being invited to provide more?

If the answer is not nearly enough then you need to work with them to improve their ability to both design and build appropriate policy and systems while building trust through providing valuable advice. A skill that is developed over time but can be helped along with good mentoring.

What's at stake? It's takes 8 hours you or your team's time to prepare to give 15 minutes of advice to a senior leader. Those 15 minutes simply can't be wasted!

So if you'd like to really dig deep on how to become a master influencer, check out my next Persuasive Adviser Course by clicking here.

Stay safe!

Cheers
Bryan

*While you may have been hired to be a trusted adviser to the executive and board, trust is earned. You are invited to become a trusted adviser by others seeking your advice. You can't simply say you are their trusted adviser.*

# Lock in Success

19 July 2022

Following on from my top three tips (see my blog 'Surprise Surprise') for you before you take up a new CRO or senior risk job offer, to avoid a nasty surprise, here are my three tips for when you start the role, to lock in your future success:

1. *Stand in the shoes of others*: As you go through your induction and learn to navigate your way around the organisation's policies, systems and its physical locations, ask yourself what it would be like for a non-risk senior manager. How is the role of risk in good governance portrayed? Would you be clear on what was expected of upper and middle managers?

2. *Be Curious*: This has two aspects to it. The first is pretty obvious. To navigate your way around the organisation you need to be naturally curious to do it well. The other angle on being curious is to "Never assume". Ask yourself and others "Why?". Why is something done a particular way? Why is it not done another way? Is it achieving its purpose?

3. *Earn Trust:* While you may have been hired to be a trusted adviser to the executive and board, trust is earned. You are invited to become a trusted adviser by others seeking your advice. You can't

simply say you are their trusted adviser. And that is why I renamed my trusted adviser program to my <u>Persuasive Advising Program</u>. You need to persuade people to take your advice so they learn to trust you!

All the best with your new role! And if my last two blogs came too late for you, it's amazing what some remedial action can do to turn things around. If you want some detailed guidance, I would encourage you to read my latest book *<u>Risky Business: How Successful Organisations Embrace Uncertainty.</u>*

Cheers
Bryan

# CHANGE MANAGEMENT

# Making Change
## 1 February 2022

In 2017 my friend and colleague Jeff Schwisow wrote in his book _Projectify:_

> "In today's business world, truly effective governance is more about having a strategy for adapting to change and variability than being able to predict the future and executing a plan that makes that prediction come true."

No one is likely to argue with that point now!

Now let me apply similar thinking to the risk function in organisations:

> In today's risk function, truly effective risk management programs are more about having a strategy to implement change than being able to quote "better practice" and execute a plan that the business does not buy into.

Are you a change maker? Digby Scott, author of Change Makers, refers to change makers as:

> "... self-driven, self-starters, who don't need hand holding, but they do value fresh perspectives, ideas and inspiration to help them make the impact they want to make."

Contrast this with one of the findings from the APRA report into the culture at CBA:

> "The risk function was also described as focusing on policy writing and correctness of frameworks over implementation and engagement with the business."

Trust me. The CBA were not alone when that was written in 2018 and they would not be alone now.

If you have designed as simple a framework as you can, your implementation plan must be designed to effect change. And you need to be a change maker. My four tips for you to drive effective change when implementing a risk management program are:

1. Stand in their shoes – You need to understand their perspective.
2. Paint them a picture – They need to see the end goal.
3. Tell them a story – They need to know how WE are going to get there.
4. Make them believe – They need to have confidence you will lead them well.

Which of these do you excel at?

Cheers
Bryan

# Wimplementation

8 February 2022

How hard are you implementing? Have you thought through implementation strategy **well**? Do you have measures in place to know how you are tracking? Or are you simply doing? If any of your answers are not positive ones, here are some tips to shift you out of wimplementation. Whether you are implementing a risk management program or any other change program.

It starts with *analysis*.

First, stakeholder analysis. You need to be very clear on who you need to influence, and which stakeholders have the most influence on what you wish to achieve. Note, it is not always the established hierarchy. Next is a PESTLE analysis to assess the environment *external to your change project*. And lastly, a capability analysis so you know which areas of the business and which support functions may need more attention than others.

Now you are ready to determine your *strategy*. The approach you are going to take. For example, are there people in the business already on board with the change required that will welcome the challenge of implementation? Or will you need to recruit influencers and turn them into a team of change makers? In risk lingo, that means set up a team of Risk Champions.

Finally, design your *measures*. How you will know you have arrived at your destination. As I proclaim in the RMIA's Enterprise Risk Management Course I designed and run, you know when you have arrived when you are seeing the behaviours you want to see and none of the ones you don't. Yes, measuring behaviours can be challenging but not insurmountable. An area I am exploring more and more with various clients as well as with my Risk Leadership Group. We meet monthly to share new ideas and experiences, be sure to check it out.

Stay safe and get strong with your implementation.

Cheers
Bryan

# Shakeholder Risk

15 February 2022

If you have been reading my last blog 'Wimplementation', you will know I have been talking about change management (in particular for risk managers).

Of course, change management means identifying and managing stakeholders. This week I facilitated a workshop that presented the perfect example of the risk that stakeholders pose if they are difficult to influence. It involved a state government agency that has become the tail-wagging-the-dog type of powerful stakeholder agency. I'll call them the "boss" agency. One with all the money and plenty of clout. Shakeholder management is needed when the tail wags the dog.

In the workshop, we worked through a range of scenarios, identified risk (way too many for everyone's liking) and finished with a plan to engage with the key people in the boss agency. Before I left the workshop I had a side conversation with two of the leaders that would be setting up a meeting with the boss agency to get their views on the risks as we see them. These leaders were great. They easily articulated how this stakeholder needed to be managed – with a bit of shakeholder management 😳:

- Engage with them early about the meeting we wish to have.

- Be very clear on the objectives we have for calling the meeting. Theirs and the boss agency's.
- Make sure the right people are in the room. From both agencies and other influencing agencies.
- Make sure we are prepared and can articulate our issues verbally and visually (e.g. process maps).
- Ensure they know what is at stake from "our" side – the decision my client agency needs to make about supporting the project in the future.

That is pretty good shakeholder change management in my view.

Stay safe and get strong with your implementation.

Cheers
Bryan

# Stop Sleeping
22 February 2022

A few blogs (see my blog 'Making Change') ago I mentioned Digby Scott's definition of a change maker:

> "... self-driven, self-starters, who don't need hand holding, but they do value fresh perspectives, ideas and inspiration to help them make the impact they want to make."

Below I align his four descriptors of people's attitudes to change from his book *Change Makers* to my four levels of descriptors of how a risk function may be perceived by the business you are trying to change. Such an interesting comparison, don't you think?

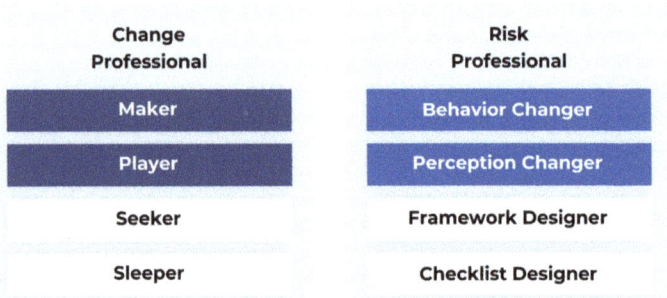

| Change Professional | Risk Professional |
|---|---|
| **Maker** | **Behavior Changer** |
| **Player** | **Perception Changer** |
| **Seeker** | **Framework Designer** |
| **Sleeper** | **Checklist Designer** |

Figure 8: Risk Advisers as Change Makers

Now you know what I mean when I say, "stop sleeping".

*I know you aren't
a sleeper and that
you've designed
a pretty good
framework and
are changing the
perceptions of some,
and the behaviours
of others. BUT ...
have you considered
yourself as a
change maker?*

I know you aren't a sleeper and that you've designed a pretty good framework and are changing the perceptions of some, and the behaviours of others. BUT ... have you considered yourself as a change maker?

If you haven't, you should! The risk profession has been working hard for decades to encourage decision makers to consider risk better than they have in the past. That means moving beyond thinking about the pros and cons of a decision, to stopping and thinking hard about some decisions. Thinking about the uncertainties and giving them a risk rating. If you don't think of yourself as a change maker, then changes won't happen. Behaviours won't change.

Have you played the game hard? Are you a now a change maker?

Stay safe and make change.

Cheers
Bryan

# Poo Poo the Poo Poo-ers

9 November 2021

My first Poo Poo the Poo Poo-ers blog was back in January 2018. I was writing about *resistors*, the Poo Poo-ers of new ideas because of reading this article from the Harvard Business Review <u>Overcome Resistance to Change with Two Conversations</u>. As it was the beginning of a new year I wrote that:

> "Right now, most people around you will be as ready for something new as they will ever be. Many are rested from a break, others took the quiet time at work to clear the decks. Now is the time to pounce. So get your team together, have the conversations, and get your year of purposeful, positive and productive change started."

The day of writing this I was talking to a leadership coach in the travel industry. We spoke about the boom the industry was about to experience and how she was working with leaders in the industry about how they were going to take advantage of the boom in new and innovative ways. We both agreed it was going to be "one hell of a ride!"

What about the rest of us? Things are happening now. Right now. Organisations, leaders and teams are re-shaping their view of the world and it is going to be one hell of a ride no matter your industry.

Many have been far from looking for something to do over the last 18 months. Many have been working tirelessly in difficult circumstances. The risk is that we let this opportunity slip because we are so exhausted.

My response was to spend a couple of days last week immersing myself in planning my next few months, setting targets, gaining focus. I'm working on blending the best of both worlds of online and in-person training as one example.

Can you muster the energy and take time to stop and plan? Do you have the energy to poo poo the poo poo-ers? I hope you do. Because it's going to be one hell of a ride!

Stay safe!

Cheers
Bryan

P.S. A byproduct from my thinking about planning is this <u>video</u> that I posted on LinkedIn about quarterly performance and risk reporting.

KPI | KRI

# Reading the Tea Leaves
### 11 May 2021

Reading the tea leaves is what most organisations are doing if they don't do Key Performance Indicators (KPIs) well. They are trying to understand the past (lag KPIs) and predict the future (lead KPIs) with nefarious measures. Measures that are either:

1. *Convenient* – Typically plucked from a list of KPIs that seem to be appropriate and subsequently deemed unimportant and are barely considered in decision making.

   *OR*

2. *Biased* – Creating an over emphasis, typically on profit in the private sector, even for organisations running a "balanced" scorecard. The result is poor decision making.

For an example of the effect of biased KPIs, look no further than the 2018-2019 Royal Commission into the Australian finance sector. The bias was towards profit and against customers, especially the least aware and the most vulnerable. In fact, we were provided with a smorgasbord of examples. There could have been no better example than that of the tellers at CBA putting a little of their own money into kids' bank accounts to meet targets set for new kids' bank accounts, thus earning themselves bonuses!

In 1956 V.F. Ridgway published a journal article titled 'Dysfunctional Consequences of Performance Measurements' and commented, "What gets measured gets managed — even when it's pointless to measure and manage it, and even if it harms the purpose of the organisation to do so."[7] Which means, the points I am making are not new, not by a long shot.

Why is this so? Because like so many things, when it comes to measurement, you have to pay attention to some of the science to get it right. You must understand what measures matter and then measure them correctly to avoid misleading statistics.

While I frequently help organisations improve their KPIs alongside my stats guru colleague Dr Andrew Pratley, I point others (who prefer a DIY approach) to my colleague Stacey Barr's PuMP training program.

Next week I will jump from KPIs to KRIs, Key Risk Indicators. If you can't wait until then, you can download Chapter 9: Reading the Signals from my book Risky Business: How Successful Organisations Embrace Uncertainty. Better still, buy my book and gain access

---

7   V.F. Ridgway. 'Dysfunctional Consequences of Performance Measurements', *Administrative Science Quarterly*, vol. 1, no. 2, September 1956, pp. 240–7.

to free resources that are there to help organisations perform better, faster!

Stay safe!

Cheers
Bryan

# Heading Them Off at the Pass

18 May 2021

I loved the movies about the Wild West of 19<sup>th</sup> Century USA when I was a kid. A favourite line from the era was "Head 'em off at the pass". Meaning, the goodies (or baddies) needed to take a short cut cross country fast to get in front of the baddies (or goodies) to surprise them and "save the day".

Key Risk Indicators (KRIs) can serve a similar purpose. Done well, they are an early indicator of things heading in the wrong direction, allowing sufficient time for an intervention to "save the day". This is the essence of outstanding risk management programs. How do I know this? Because the ex-CEO of Telstra, David Thodey, told me so.

I was at a UNSW Business School seminar where David Thodey, then CEO of Telstra, was interviewed by Narelle Hooper, then Editor of AFR BOSS magazine, in front of about 400 people. Thodey was asked a question along these lines: "What is the greatest challenge in running an organisation the size of Telstra?" (which then had over 45,000 employees). Thodey answered (in my words):

*Getting information I need to know from the extremities of the organisation, to me, past all the information people are trying to tell me, that I don't need to know, in time for me to do something about it!*

When I work with organisations to identify KRIs I always start with KPIs. However, as I pointed out last week in Reading the Tea Leaves, most organisations don't do KPIs well. Which makes it difficult to have good KRIs. So, the first step is identifying what really matters and how to measure that correctly. Once you have identified those measures you can identify their key drivers of uncertainty and determine how best to measure them correctly. These become your KRIs.

In general, when it comes to KPIs and KRIs, less is more and I tend to operate fairly high up in the organisation with KRIs and leave it as KPIs for lower down management. At least while the maturity of the organisation (when it comes to managing risk) is building.

To read more on KRIs you can download Chapter 9: Reading the Signals from my book *Risky Business: How Successful Organisations Embrace Uncertainty*. Better still, buy my book and gain access to free resources that are there to help organisations perform better, faster!

Stay safe!

Cheers
Bryan

# KRISS or KISS

13 September 2022

KRISS doesn't stand for anything relating to risk that I am aware of. I just made it up to get you to read this blog on how to develop Key Risk Indicators. Sorry. KISS stands for "Keep It Simple, Stupid."

When I work with organisations to help them develop KRIs I use the KISS principle. Because it is way different to the alternative. The alternative is a long list of KRIs that take up staff time to develop monitoring and reporting processes. All with questionable value, especially if your organisation's Key Performance Indicators (KPIs) are crap as I wrote about two weeks ago in <u>Reading the tea leaves</u>.

Last week in <u>Heading them off at the pass</u>, I wrote that your KRIs come from your KPIs and to get the KPIs sorted first. That is the beginning of the KISS principle. Don't create a whole new separate world. Make sure it is all linked to the uncertainty of achieving objectives.

Next, apply the 7+/-2 <u>principle</u> which is that we humble humans can only focus on five to nine things at a time. If I was to give you 27 KPIs for the year, you would have no chance of remembering them. However, if I gave you 5 KPIs containing those 27 you could remember the 5 and for the one you're most concerned about, you could name the 5 or so items that make it up.

Applying that to KRIs, you can have a KRI for customer service based on a number of sub-KRIs like 'wait times' or '% of complaints resolved within a period of time'.

One way of working out which sub-KRIs you should be caring about the most is to prepare a customer service risk profile. This will lead you to identify the key drivers of uncertainty (risks) and the controls being relied on. For example, having KPIs for wait teams for call centre staff.

If customer service is something you are focusing on (and by the way all risk teams should be focused on their own customer service), I highly recommend Service Mindset by Jaquie Scammell. It even has an endorsement from David Thodey, ex CEO of Telstra, who I wrote about last week in Heading them off at the pass.

To read more on KRIs you can download Chapter 9: Reading the Signals from my book *Risky Business: How Successful Organisations Embrace Uncertainty*. Better still, buy my book and gain access to free resources that are there to help organisations perform better, faster!

Stay safe!

Cheers
Bryan

# QUANTIFICATION

# Accuracy over Buckshot

7 July 2020

*WARNING – If you are a vegetarian, vegan or an animal lover you may be offended by the story in this blog.*

When you're presented with numbers you don't know if they are buckshot or accurate. You often assume the later when it is often the former.

You must often witness people plucking out of thin air, numbers such as budget estimates, estimates of probability and estimates of impact. It is very common because it takes time to get accurate. We often prefer the buckshot approach because we hit some part of the target. Unfortunately, the bigger the beast, the bigger the mistake to be firing buckshot.

My brother-in-law – who lives in the Yukon Territory, Canada – hunts annually for the family's yearly meat supply. When he hunts large beasts like buffalo, he does not use buckshot. He relies on his finely-honed shooting skills and his precision equipment to down what is a massive animal. And he does it with one shot. Better for the animal and better for the quality of the meat.

In the past few weeks I have been speaking with my esteemed stats guru, friend and colleague who lectures at the University of Sydney Business School, Dr

Andrew Pratley, about this tendency towards buckshot at the cost of accuracy. I raised with him the extent of Quantifornication (my word for the plucking of numbers out of thin air) that I see in business, in particular when people are trying to estimate really uncertain things. Like scenario planning during COVID!

Our discussion quickly turned to how easy it is to improve estimates in everyday business. Next thing you know we are on a mission to take on Quantifornication. Next week will be the start of a series co-written with Dr Pratley.

Stay safe and adapt – with better measurement!

Cheers
Bryan

# Pointed Estimates
14 July 2020

*My stats guru colleague Dr Andrew Pratley and I are on the move to tackle Quantifornication (see my blog 'Accuracy over Buckshot), the **plucking of numbers out of thin air**. Here is the first in a series co-written together.*

One of the biggest problems with estimates is that it takes a long time to find out if you were right. A year for a budget, two, three or more years for a strategy. Political polling is the best example of being able to assess if the estimate was correct. On election night – and we all know how that has been going lately.

One scenario we have been working on is cyber security to answer the question, how much cyber security is enough? Or, better still, what is the risk?

There are two broad extremes which are worth starting from: do nothing, spend no money and hope for the best; or do everything, have an unlimited budget and know you're safe. The value of extreme positions is not to advocate for one or the other but to place markers. The current theory is that the more you spend, the more you can do and therefore the safer you are.

Let's test this out. If you had a house with ten entrances and you could only spend money to secure seven of these, in theory, you'd be safer than someone that could only secure three of the entrances. This statement is only true if you assume that every entrance is equally likely to be used to break-in. This assumption is rarely true, even when it seems entirely reasonable. The reason is explained via the Monty Hall problem:

> *Suppose you're on a game show, and you're given the choice of three doors: behind one door is a car; behind the others, goats. You pick a door, say No. 1, and the host, who knows what's behind the doors, opens another door, say No. 3, which has a goat. He then says to you, "Do you want to pick door No. 2?" Is it to your advantage to switch your choice?*

When presented with this seemingly straightforward problem, the vast majority of people choose to keep their selection. They end up disappointed and go home with a goat (watch this YouTube video entitled 'The Monty Hall Problem – Explained'.)

Our message to you is that not everything is what it seems and that you should be making more accurate assessments. Next week we will discuss how to calculate more accurate estimates, what statisticians call point estimates. Quite different to guesses!

Stay safe and adapt – with better measurement!

Cheers
Bryan

# The Danger of the Guessing Game

21 July 2020

*My stats guru colleague Dr Andrew Pratley and I are on the move to tackle <u>Quantifornication</u>, the **plucking of numbers out of thin air**. Here is the second in a series we are co-writing.*

We're far better at identifying good and bad writing than we are identifying good and bad numbers. The premise of this idea almost doesn't seem logical. How can a language like English, with all of its oddities, be easier to separate the good from the bad?

Our education in English has a substantial amount of time devoted to comparing different types of writing and methods to improve readability and comprehension. We accept and understand there is no 'right way' and don't become fixated on this idea. Almost all of our number education focuses on calculations to get the right answer. We rarely discuss where the numbers come from, or their validity.

When we talk about numbers we tend to assume we're discussing clear and agreeable ideas such as the temperature in a room (19°C), our height without shoes on (1,820mm) or the number of customers that visit the store in a day (65). These are fairly easy to check. In the same way, as each of these three scenarios generates a specific value, we can generate specific values for the predicted maximum temperature tomorrow, the predicted height of a child when they turn 18 or the number of customers we think will make a purchase tomorrow.

While we inherently know the 'weatherman' is not always right, and that the height of a child and the number of buyers are only predictions, it is how we treat this information that is important. In some instances, we will treat the information with caution. Some of us will take something warm in case the temperature is a few degrees cooler than predicted. And for something like the height of a child, the timeline for realisation of that prediction is so far out, we give it little consideration – like many have with climate change. And for the number of customers we think will make a purchase tomorrow, we make decisions on staffing and inventory.

This last example of customers is an example of how we tend to intermix reliable numbers (the measured number of customers in the store) with what are normally unreliable numbers (the estimated number of customers purchasing). While temperature estimates are based on sophisticated modelling with estimated margins of error, the estimate of customer purchases is usually an educated guess unless you work for a company that has invested in analytics AND run the numbers with statistical validity.

The reality is that many of the important decisions we

make every day are based on guesstimates that we like to believe are more accurate than they are. We think they are "point estimates" in statistician-speak.

Statisticians are always talking about point estimates. Our conversations with each other involve qualifiers like "Do we have a representative sample?", "Have we accounted for a particular bias?" Statisticians know the danger of playing the guessing game when making important decisions about investing, resourcing and prioritising projects.

The old saying – "There are lies, damn lies and statistics" should really be rephrased to – "There are lies, damned lies and guesstimates".

Now we're set up for next week where we will write about how to move from guestimates to point estimates for improved decision making.

Stay safe and adapt – with better measurement!

Cheers
Bryan

*The old saying –*
*"There are lies, damn*
*lies and statistics"*
*should really be*
*rephrased to – "There*
*are lies, damned lies*
*and guesstimates".*

# From Guestimate to Estimate – as Simple as 1, 2, 3

28 July 2020

*My stats guru colleague Dr Andrew Pratley and I are on the move to tackle <u>Quantifornication</u>, the **plucking of numbers out of thin air**. Here is the third in a series we are co-writing.*

For most people that have had to sit through an entire class of statistics, you'd reasonably assume the staff are sadistic and enjoy seeing people fall asleep, and slowly stop turning up. If you met the staff outside of this context you'd never pick them to teach this subject. Like most educators, they're passionate and spend considerable time and effort trying to explain the ideas.

Why do so many educators in statistics consistently fail to translate these ideas into something that people can both remember and use? The problem is the language, not the numbers. Part of the problem with statistics, as is the case with most technical subjects, is the unique terminology. The COVID-19 pandemic has shown us many things, one unexpected outcome was the mainstream discussion of distributions, as in "we must flatten the curve!" Distributions are the basis of statistics.

Whilst there is a learning curve to the terminology, most

of us are left with a dizzying array of formulas, methods and tables to work out how to use. None of which make sense outside of a specific context. So let us help you.

Statistics answers three types of questions:

1. Questions about probability.
2. Questions about differences.
3. Questions about relationships.

Everything that will transform our lives in the next 20 years through the application of machine learning and AI uses a combination of these three approaches.

What's hard to see is how the problem you might want to solve fits into one of these three categories. Because we learn to use formulas, we don't have the chance to explore and play around with these ideas.

This three-question framework application to risk professionals is easiest seen through the risk matrix. We all know the shortcomings of the technique, but how do we use statistics to improve our ability to make decisions? The risk matrix has two axes – likelihood and consequence and a third aspect, control and treatment measures to manage or mitigate risk.

Using the three types of questions framework we could link:

1. **Questions about probability to the likelihood axis.**

   We could use the method of probability to improve our estimate of the likelihood of a successful cyber attack. To do this we might use the binomial distribution to model the number of active threats.

2. **Questions about differences to control measures.**

   We could use the method of differences to determine if one control measure is more effective than another. To do this we might run a two-sample t-test comparing a spam filter to a compulsory online learning module.

3. **Questions about relationships to any of (i) likelihood & consequence (ii) likelihood & control measures or (iii) consequence & control measures.**

We could use the method of relationships to determine if there is a relationship between control measures and likelihood. To do this we might run a regression analysis to see if spending more money on control measures actually reduces the likelihood of the risk occurring.

Risk professionals are asking these types of questions all

the time. We believe that by creating the link between the questions we ask and the three-question framework above we can all make better decisions in uncertain times.

Stay safe and adapt – with better measurement!

Cheers
Bryan

# Infinite Possibilities Is Not the Trap
## 4 August 2020

*My stats guru colleague Dr Andrew Pratley and I are on the move to tackle <u>Quantifornication</u>, the **plucking of numbers out of thin air**. Here is the fourth in a series we are co-writing.*

We all have a tendency to overestimate our knowledge. And as a result, we believe that we know things which we don't. Our understanding of what is random is even worse – hence Nassim Taleb's book <u>Fooled by Randomness.</u> It's the overconfidence that is the problem. It causes us to jump to the wrong answer and believe it is right.

Let's take an example of something that we all 'know'. If I rolled a die and a six came up you'd think that's unremarkable. If I rolled another six you'd think that reasonable. If I continued to roll six after six; three, four or five times in a row you'd be convinced that I was cheating, that the die was loaded or there was something wrong. We all know the chance of a six is 1/6. What's hard to imagine is that it's entirely possible, even if incredibly unlikely, not just to roll five sixes (with a probability of 1/7776) but to roll a million sixes in a row on a fair die. Actually it is entirely possible to role a six an infinite number of times.

How is your head?

The very idea of infinity is not something we can grasp. There's no mental model that makes sense, no set of rules or structures we can rely on.

Irrespective, we are always looking for rules or guidelines to understand the world when it comes to probability. This focus often doesn't serve us. Knowing the probability of five sixes in a row is 1/7776, we generalise this to mean that if we conduct this experiment 7,776 times, we should see this result once. That's not true. The actual outcome will be somewhere in a distribution of outcomes ranging from 0 to 7,776. This simple example shows we tend to talk about probability as though these are fixed outcomes, but they exist on a distribution, a distribution that is very difficult to grasp when we are seeking rules and guidelines.

How do we apply these ideas to improving estimates of likelihood? The first and most important idea is not to see probability as a fixed outcome. A once in a hundred-year flood doesn't happen every hundred years, it happens when a specific set of circumstances occur. Understanding and quantifying these circumstances will be more useful than thinking the probability is 1/100 because we gain understanding of the key drivers and can create early warning signals so we can prepare for the highly unlikely event. Signals you might refer to as Key Risk Indicators.

*When we have
better estimates
of likelihood of a
risk occurring, we
need to hold onto
them lightly and be
responsive to new
information, not
dogmatic in our
beliefs about data.*

The second idea is that most of what we're interested in doesn't follow predictable probabilities such as rolling dice and flipping coins. So if we are going to improve decision making we need to find better ways to make more accurate estimates of probability than plucking numbers out of thin air in a workshop. That's right. Quantifornication.

When we have better estimates of likelihood of a risk occurring, we need to hold onto them lightly and be responsive to new information, not dogmatic in our beliefs about data. When we're driving on a rough road, we want to use the feedback through the steering wheel to guide us, not spend all our time and effort ignoring the signals and fighting against the conditions.

Stay safe and adapt – with better measurement!

Cheers
Bryan

# Taste Testing Quantification
## 11 August 2020

*My stats guru colleague Dr Andrew Pratley and I are on the move to tackle Quantifornication, the **plucking of numbers out of thin air**. Here is the fifth in a series we are co-writing.*

The story of statistics started with a question about differences (see my blog 'From Guestimate to Estimate – As simple as 1,2,3'). R.A. Fisher set out to test if someone really could taste the difference between tea where the milk was poured in before or after the tea. Fisher's experimental design was simple. Eight cups of tea were prepared, four with the milk poured before, four with the milk poured after. Four were presented to Muriel Bristol in a random order. The lady correctly identified all four cups and Fisher came up with the mathematics to show that this result was extremely unlikely to occur by chance. The mathematics behind this became known as Fisher's exact test.

Fisher went on to study crops and provided the framework for much of what we use today. The questions Fisher answered were related to many of the questions we're interested in today. Fisher wanted to know if one type of fertiliser promoted faster crop growth than another. Or if the way the crops were planted impacted their growth, or the amount of water provided changed the yield. By understanding these, Fisher was able to determine how to make the best decision, when choices are available, based on statistical analysis.

All business leaders are making decisions between different approaches. *Critically, and fortunately for us, we don't need to be capable of developing statistical methods like Fisher, we just need to be able to apply them.* While Fisher used pencil, pad and slide-rule, business leaders today have access to 90 years of research and development that are pretty well captured in Microsoft Excel.

The opportunity for professionals like you is to develop the ability to see situations and identify how statistical methods could be used. We tend to think statistics only apply to large data sets full of numbers. As the example at the start showed, Fisher was able to test if someone could tell the difference in how tea was prepared. Which informs people on how best to make tea for those who like the taste with the milk poured before or after. Fisher accomplished this without collecting a single number.

The questions you answer on differences could well be more profound and important than how to pour tea to your liking (unless you really like tea), but the underlying ideas remain the same. Statistical analysis doesn't have to be something relegated to the too hard basket in the favour of other less accurate methods.

Stay safe and adapt – with better measurement!

Cheers
Bryan

# Testing Relationships
18 August 2020

*My stats guru colleague Dr Andrew Pratley and I are on the move to tackle <u>Quantifornication</u>, the **plucking of numbers out of thin air**. Here is the sixth in a series we are co-writing.*

Relationships are the branch of statistics that describe how one thing influences another. We know these as regression analysis, x-y plots or scatter plots. The classic regression plot involves a line of best fit. We tend to think that the better the line of fit, the better the statistical relationship. That's true, but it's not the entire story.

Just like in our lives, (statistical) relationships are complex and often hard to interpret. We tend to fall back on rules of thumb, rather than really understanding what we're trying to do. The point of relationships in statistics is the belief that we have something relatively cheap and easy that is a good predictor of something we're interested in that is complex, difficult and time-consuming. We need both of these to be true for statistical relationships to be worth pursuing.

Take early childhood education for example. Until the data was collected and analysed, many parents would have suspected that investing in their child's early education was for the better but could not be sure because life outcomes are complex. We now know that time, effort and money put into a child before they start school has a profound impact on their education level and achievement (<u>OECD</u>). Ask parents about the money they'll spend on their child's education and some may respond that they're saving for a private school for high school or possibly university. One of the challenges with relationships is appreciating the time over which they occur. It's arguably one of the primary reasons for compulsory superannuation. We simply can't look far enough ahead to understand the benefits of what we're doing today.

In case you're wondering why early childhood learning is so valuable it's a combination of the rate of brain development (that slows down over time) and that learning early creates the ability to become a better learner. In an optimal world, we'd spend every dollar and minute we have developing children before they enter kindergarten. This investment compounds in the same way early contributions to superannuation do.

In risk management, there are a number of statistical relationships that might be of interest; such as the relationship between control measures and likelihood. What we'd like to see is that by implementing a control measure we reduce the likelihood of something happening. For example, we should be interested in the relationship between cybersecurity training and the likelihood of a breach. However, we rarely objectively measure the value of training. But if we did, what we'd want to see is that for each session staff attend, two outcomes occur.

First, we'd hope to see staff being more cautious about clicking on links and secondly, we'd hope to see this sustained beyond just a short period of time. A strong relationship between the training and the intended outcomes, less likelihood of a successful phishing attack, would mean we could be clear on the optimal investment in training. And the optimal investment in training could be determined by asking the question: "How much training do I need to reduce the likelihood of a cyber breach from phishing attacks to a level of x per annum per thousand employees?"

If we found that the amount of training didn't have a relationship to reducing the likelihood, then it's possible that we have an ineffective control measure.

Stay safe and adapt – with better measurement!

Cheers
Bryan

# When Uncertain, Seek Directionality
## 25 August 2020

*My stats guru colleague Dr Andrew Pratley and I are on the move to tackle <u>Quantifornication</u>, the **plucking of numbers out of thin air**. Here is the seventh in a series we are co-writing.*

Nothing is certain. Not even death and taxes. Because the only certainty is uncertainty, there's no foolproof way to make the right decision. Most organisations deal with this by putting in a time constraint. Forcing a decision, however imperfect it may be.

While keeping the organisation moving by forcing decisions is admirable, the organisations we work with that prove most successful also look to improve the information available. Some high-level research, some investigation of data or similar. However, few do the hard-smart work that Andrew and I help organisations do. We create hypotheses and then test them harder and harder over time. Andrew calls this directionality. Directionality can be thought of as a vector. It has both direction and magnitude. The value of using directionality is that it leads us to better decisions by assuming we are making the right decision and testing it over time.

Much of the current approach with regard to quantifying

uncertainty in risk management is about developing calibrated ranges, based on guessing values and then simulating the results. This is a vast improvement over just guessing a value and then hoping it's right, or wrong. What this approach misses is that we're trying to avoid uncertainty by creating artificial distinctions. Using this approach is like drawing state borders in countries. Lines on a map are fine until things go wrong. All of sudden we find that this approach splits up families, stops access to medical care and stops kids going to school. Things we never saw until we started relying on this knowledge.

Directionality embraces the underlying uncertainty. What we work towards is seeing how our understanding changes based on additional information. The simplest example of this is how we can infer more about a decision by conducting a survey. The amount of directionality is related to the sample size we select.

Let's take an example where we want to know if we should return to working from the office next month. We ask one person and they say "Yes". That's 100% agreement with returning to the office. Would you re-sign the lease based on this? Of course not. If you had the same result from a group of ten, you'd be a bit more inclined. If from a group of 100, this would be hard to ignore. If you asked every single person and they all said yes, you'd know what to do. The strength of this or the directionality is proportional to the sample size. There's no right sample size but finding the same result over a larger group gives a greater sense of directionality. Statistics show this to be true by reducing the size of the confidence interval.

The value of sampling is to increase your confidence in a decision without committing to a belief that you can't change your mind, or trying to create a world that is not inherently uncertain. If we ever needed evidence of the underlying uncertainty, 2020 has shown us this in a way, few could have ever imagined.

This concludes the series I have written jointly with Andrew on defeating Quantifornication. I hope we have got you thinking and you are planning your next steps to improve decision making in your organisation.

Stay safe and adapt – with better measurement!

Cheers
Bryan

# Finding Directionality
1 September 2020

*My stats guru colleague Dr Andrew Pratley and I are on the move to tackle <u>Quantifornication</u>, the **plucking of numbers out of thin air**. Last week was supposed to be our final blog we are co-writing but we couldn't resist sneaking in another one after the great response from our last one.*

Last week we wrote about the concept of directionality (see my blog '<u>When uncertain, seek directionality</u>'), taking what you know having applied the three-question framework (also from my blog '<u>From Guestimate to Estimate – As simple as 1,2,3</u>') and testing with more data to gain even more certainty of your decisions. We defined directionality to be a vector, meaning it has both direction and magnitude. We described how surveying one person, then ten then a larger group (each time getting the same result) means you can be more confident in the data. 50% from a group of 10 people has less strength than 50% from a group of 1000.

However, many of the questions we're trying to answer or decisions we're trying to make often don't have easily accessible data sets. One approach is to ask experts to guess, but unfortunately, experts often aren't that much better than the layperson.

Using the idea of directionality, we could approach things

*Using the concept of directionality we could begin to measure what we believe has a direct causal link to the likelihood of a catastrophic explosion.*

differently. Instead of trying to estimate what we're interested in by guessing the value, we could measure a range of other variables that are causally related and use these to build a simple model based on objective data.

This is not a new idea, psychology has had to develop approaches to this. We can't actually measure the IQ of someone, what we do is measure specific attributes and use these to make an estimate. Those attributes happen to be language, numeracy and spatial patterns, hence why these feature heavily in IQ tests.

Returning to risk, let's take the example of a catastrophic explosion at an oil refinery. We know these happen, and that the likelihood across the industry is low. Experts might make estimates based on the age of the refinery and by looking around at the systems and staff.

Could we do better? Using the concept of directionality we could begin to measure what we believe has a direct causal link to the likelihood of a catastrophic explosion. We could measure the amount spent on maintenance versus the required amount and look at this over the preceding years. We could look at the shift patterns and know that longer shifts result in more operator errors. We could look at the handover procedures and tagging system. We could measure the attitude of senior management towards hitting production targets as compared to safety.

We know that as these increase (the gap between the

money required and spent, the length of shifts and the desire to hit production targets) they all contribute to increasing the likelihood of a catastrophic explosion. We could also find variables that as they increase, decrease the likelihood. This might include training and the experience of the operators.

The use of expert judgement is to weigh which of these variables has the most impact, instead of guessing the values. By developing this approach you can directly link the model to the control measures. Building a model with a number of verifiable inputs is more likely to give an accurate estimate than using a small number of experts to guess what they think will happen.

Stay safe and adapt – with better measurement!

Cheers
Bryan

# Data Problems Are Not the Real Problem

8 September 2020

My colleague Dr Andrew Pratley and I are on a mission to defeat Quantifornication. Last week we ran the first of two free interactive webinars we are running to explore the topic. We had attendees from a range of industries including banking, emergency services, energy, insurance, health, policy agencies and regulators from federal and state governments, local government, engineering consultants, risk and cyber risk consultants, IT service providers and many more.

Everyone was there for the same reason. Their discomfort with the acceptance of Quantifornication. How does Quantifornication come about? To answer that question I must quote one of the attendees who introduced me to the acronym BOGSAT. Which stands for Bunch of Guys Sitting Around Talking. What worried him the most was that in his field he applies it to military security risks where the consequences of events can be fatal and frequently are.

During the session I commented that most of my clients that embarked on, or are on big data projects, spent a heap of money and utilised a heap of resources for well more than a year before they could even smell the hint of some real benefit. Why? Because people think they need bucket loads of data to solve problems.

One of my favourite lines Andrew has given me is: "It's not about big data, it's about your data". When I said that to the attendees, there was a pause and then the questions flowed:

- What data do I need?
- How much data is enough?

What's most interesting is that these are not even the right questions to ask. The better question is:

- What is the problem I am trying to solve?

When you know the problem you want to solve, you can then either identify the data that may help you answer the question or, as described in my blog (Taste Testing Quantification) about R.A. Fisher in the 1930s, design an experiment from which data is created. An experiment known as The Lady Testing Tea.

Let me leave you with this final comment by one of the participants:

> "We have lots and lots of data. What we found from the recent bushfire season is that we didn't have any of the right data."

It's not about big data. It's about articulating the problem you need to solve and working from there.

Stay safe and adapt – with better measurement!

Cheers
Bryan

# Escaping the Matrix!

15 September 2020

A key takeaway for attendees at the free interactive webinars I am running with my colleague Dr Andrew Pratley on Quantifornication was that when it comes to the field of risk assessment, scrapping the risk matrix is not the first step you should take.

There are many, many risk practitioners who are calling for the scrapping of the risk matrix. When I run the RMIA's Enterprise Risk Management course I ask participants why the risk matrix came into being. The answer is to navigate a path between two people arguing as to whether a risk is too high to take or not. The risk matrix gives a definition of risk levels based on assessed levels of likelihood and consequence and pre-defined risk criteria. If you are accurate in your assessment of likelihood and consequence and your risk criteria is appropriate for your appetite for risk, it is a good tool for decision making.

So what is the problem?

The problem is that the assessments of likelihood and consequence are simply wrong or misleading. They are either plucked out of thin air or are not presented with information about the underlying probability distributions.

So don't scrap the risk matrix just yet. People are used to it, it facilitates great conversations that need to be had and it can be used as the starting point of getting accurate with risk analysis. Andrew and I are simply suggesting that you take one of your higher risks on your risk heat map and start asking the right questions about the underlying problem. Is it likelihood that we really don't understand, or consequence, or both. Do we have a lack of understanding of the reliability and effectiveness of controls?

When you identify one or more problems you can start a journey to getting accurate with risk analysis using the three-question framework Andrew and I introduced you to in our blog <u>From Guestimate to Estimate – As simple as 1, 2, 3.</u>

Stay safe and adapt – with better measurement!

Cheers
Bryan

# Early Indications Are ...
22 September 2020

Where should your lead indicators (KRIs or Key Risk Indicators in the field of risk) come from?

A few years ago my colleague Andrew Pratley and I toured the country to speak at Chartered Accountants Business Forums. We spoke on KPIs – Key Performance Indicators. We talked about lead and lag indicators and we talked about limiting the number of KPIs, as having too many creates its own industry of measurement and reporting with very little influence on decision making. Because more often than not organisations are not measuring enough of the measures that really matter.

The answer to identifying the lead indicators (or KRIs) you should be measuring are best identified after you have a very clear understanding of the drivers of what is important to you. If your organisation has identified its strategic risks, you likely have some high risks on a heat map. If you have high risks, presumably they are important to you. And if you follow my suggestion from last week's <u>Escaping the Matrix!</u> blog you will be working on developing real clarity on what is driving the likelihood or consequence (or both) for one or more of your high risks. You should also be seeking clarity on the controls being relied upon to manage the risk. Are they reliable and effective when being deployed?

*If your organisation has identified its strategic risks, you likely have some high risks on a heat map.*

In amongst this analysis you will find one or two really important lead indicators you should be monitoring to give an early warning of this risk evolving into a risk event. For example, when it comes to safety in higher hazard industries, the one thing that matters the most is the level of engagement of senior management in conversations about safety. Staff take safety very seriously if senior management take it very seriously. Measuring the number and quality of senior management site safety visits would be a very good indicator, months in advance, of how your safety record will be trending.

Stay safe and adapt – with better measurement!

Cheers
Bryan

# Getting Under the Skin of Mr Assume

29 September 2020

Back in 2015, McKinsey published a paper on <u>The future of risk management in the banking sector</u>. At the time I sent it to many of my clients in other sectors because of its very important messages, including this one in their summary:

> *"Bank risk management will likely look dramatically different by 2025, when it has become a core part of banks' strategic planning, a close collaborator with business heads, and a centre of excellence in analytics and de-biased decision making."*

The paper includes commentary on how advanced banks were digitising, using machine learning, for example to improve decision making in relation to loans and the potential for default. Since then, Australia has seen a Royal Commission into the finance sector with a well-documented focus on non-financial risk.

While a digital strategy is important to any organisation if you want to de-bias decision making, what about the bias in decision making where there is a lack of data? The answer is to test underlying assumptions by forming a hypothesis and testing that hypothesis by collecting data. And the data you need may not be far away.

An example might be that you have experienced high turnover in a particular professional skill set in your industry with salaries rising steeply and the ability to even find staff falling just as steeply. The prevailing view is that the cause of the problem is a lack of new graduates over recent years. A fair assumption. But only an assumption. It could also be that graduates are in demand in new industries for example.

This would be relatively easy to test by obtaining the numbers of graduates from universities over the past 5 years. There may also be data about where those graduates have ended up and there might be correlations between which industries/companies are presenting at the graduate employment career fairs. Knowing what the cause is gives you a better understanding of how long and how severe the lack of graduates may be. And potentially what to do about it.

All this without using deeper research skills employing statistical methods. Depending on the scale of your problem, deeper research may well be worth it.

Stay safe and adapt – with better measurement!

Cheers
Bryan

# Nudging the CFO
6 October 2020

Can you make a difference with measurement if the culture of your organisation is one that does not respect, let alone crave data? In my experience it is tough to go hard against the grain of an organisation's culture. The better way is to nudge it.

How might you nudge it? Culture change can start from outside the executive team but ultimately it has to be adopted by a key executive and then the whole executive. So no better place to start than with the strategic risks of your organisation.

How do you start? One way is to approach the CFO and ask them how they view the strategic risk profile of the organisation affecting decisions about the balance sheet. That is, how much capital is being tied up because of the burden of risk. The burden that falls upon decision makers that leads them to hold something in reserve in case things don't turn out as planned.

The next question to ask is what would it mean to the CFO if they had more certainty about the financial risk of the strategic risk profile. If capital could potentially be freed up. Or if they could explain with more evidence to the executive and the board why their advice is to hold a certain level of reserves.

If the answers are positive, then together choose one of the organisation's strategic risks that has uncertain financial impact that the CFO would like to be more certain about and start Escaping the Matrix!; my blog about using statistical methods to better understand risks subjectively placed on the risk matrix.

An example for an airline like Qantas or Virgin before COVID would be the risk of a new entrant into the profitable domestic market. On the face of it, hard to estimate. However, there is data you could seek out. How many airlines in the world have the financial capacity, the fleet capacity (or more likely over capacity), the trend in regulation of the industry. Once things are in a new normal for the airline industry, they will have plenty of data about financial shocks and different strategies with which to respond!

So go give your CFO a nudge with something that really speaks to them.

Stay safe and adapt – with better measurement!

Cheers
Bryan

# Beyond Nudging
13 October 2020

Sometimes you need to go beyond <u>nudging decision makers.</u> However, the personal risk you take when challenging a decision depends on culture.

Last week I was given cause to reflect on my time at HIH Insurance and the causes of its demise in 2001. While there were many, and people with different lenses could easily come to different conclusions, my view is that the culture did not allow sufficient leaders to speak their mind.

The CEO, Ray Williams, was a powerful personality. One of the most caring, thoughtful and engaging leaders I have experienced. He was able to inspire belief in the mission. Unfortunately, he was so good, it was not part of the culture of the organisation to criticise him.

Ray also put great trust in his senior leaders. Many had been with him for more than two decades. And without the checks and balances now expected in modern insurance companies, one senior leader after another were able to dig themselves into a financial hole that ultimately the organisation could not dig itself out.

Many risk professionals see their job as one of 'oversight and challenge'. My message to them is, unless you have a very mature culture where the psychological safety exists for open and consequence-free questioning of decision makers, stating that your role is to oversee and challenge makes your job more difficult. I say to them:

> "Senior leaders like being challenged ... when proven right! And nobody on this planet likes to be 'oversighted'!"

So instead of having the difficult conversation decision after decision, a smarter approach is to have one big conversation about the extent that psychological safety exists in the organisation so people can raise their voices, be heard and feel safe to do so.

Stay safe and adapt.

Cheers
Bryan

# Nudging Executives
20 October 2020

Senior leaders love to be challenged when you prove them right!

Unfair? Yes. There are plenty of great leaders who truly want their staff to speak up. However, even some of these may suffer from measurement blindness.

When it comes to numbers and decision making there are three positions people take.

## Believers

These people believe measurement enhances decisions. They will ask for measurement and readily listen to the numbers being presented, they will look to see if there are any abnormalities and when satisfied, they will trust the numbers.

## Swingers

These are the people that like the numbers when it suits them and not so when they don't. They will accept data that affirms their position, and they will reject data that goes against their conclusions.

## Gamblers

These are the gut feel decision makers. The ones that follow the mantra that there are three types of lies: "Lies, damned lies and statistics". They simply don't believe what comes from a 'black box'.

When <u>nudging the CFO,</u> presumably they are believers in measurement. When nudging other executives, it is important to understand if they are a believer, a swinger or a gambler.

For believers your mantra should be "If you can observe it, I can measure it, but I'll closely consider the cost of measurement along the way."

For swingers and gamblers, your mantra should be "I can give you some further insight to help you with this decision." That is, don't talk data and measurement, talk insights. The marketing insights teams worked that one out many years ago.

Stay safe and adapt – with better measurement!

Cheers
Bryan

# Hating Restraints
27 October 2020

People mostly don't like to be restrained. We also don't like some constraints but we like others. For example, we like choice when buying but we don't like too many choices.

Restraints on the other hand are an attack on our freedom.

Take seat belts for example. They were first <u>invented the century before last</u>! The modern retractable 3-point seat belt was invented in the 1950s. However, seat belt wearing was not compulsory and it took government legislation, regulation and enforcement to get more than a minority of people to use them. Now that generations are being raised with the act of buckling up coming naturally to them, utilisation rates have reached very high levels. It no longer feels like a constraint on our freedom.

For some people, using measurement in decision making interferes with their freedom of choice. Measurement is a restraint.

One option to tackle this is to make measurement compulsory, like governments did with seat belts. And many organisations have. But many, many others have not.

Another option is to give senior decision makers the

freedom they desire. Don't present your advice and associated evidence, measured data, as providing THE answer. Provide it as a range of possible outcomes with various options.

Provided with the freedom to choose, decision makers are likely to act more rationally and be more fully behind the decision.

Stay safe and adapt – with better measurement!

Cheers
Bryan

# Optify Your Advice
3 November 2020

"Provided with the freedom to choose, decision makers are likely to act more rationally and be more fully behind the decision." Is how I finished last week's blog, 'Hating Restraints'.

Optifying your advice is delivering the freedom to choose in the optimum way. Your optimum way. And it follows the Rule of Three.

People like things in threes. Think of The Three Little Pigs or The Three Musketeers or Superman's: 'Truth, justice and the American way'. Or Shakespeare's Julius Caesar: 'Friends, Romans, Countrymen'; or advertisers: 'Slip, Slop, Slap' (a very successful government-funded campaign in Australia in the 1980s to shift people's attitudes to taking precautions against skin cancer).

We like things in threes. We just do.

So optimise your advice using the rule of three. For most complex or at least complicated decisions there are multiple options that can be taken. Prepare three when giving your advice.

One should be low end, not favoured by you but at least heading in the right direction. One should be high-end. You would be over the moon if that option is taken. And one should be in a sweet spot in the middle. People like choice and will more likely be swayed away from the low-end to the middle by the high-end choice.

So when presenting the findings from your measurement of data, provide it as a range as best you can and give three options across the range.

Stay safe and adapt – with better measurement!

Cheers
Bryan

# Finally I Get Stats 101
10 November 2020

I don't know if you have noticed, but I have been blogging about measurement, data, and statistics for the past 19 weeks. All to defeat Quantifornication – the act of pulling numbers out of thin air for decision making. Numbers that are seemingly reliable but are not.

This week I presented with my colleague Dr Andrew Pratley: Statistics 101 Applied to Controls – How to test and measure control resilience. Our presentation was part of the RMIA and AISA Risk & Cyber Week conference. We only had 25 minutes and so we made the call to prepare case studies for people attending the presentation, to have somewhere to go to dig into these concepts, for a proper understanding of the value of statistics.

Andrew and I have recorded near on an hour of video (watch the 'RMIA Risk & Cyber Week 2020: Statistics 101 Applied to Controls'), explaining three examples of how to use statistics for assessing cyber security controls.

But here is the kick. I am a chemical engineer with an MBA. I did Statistics in engineering and in my MBA. Did I understand it? Enough to pass but not enough to do anything practical with it. Andrew has long said that the way Statistics is taught is entirely unconducive to gaining the in-depth understanding needed to apply it.

You will see in each of the three case studies, that Andrew describes the control test and the data created from it. He then, in just a few minutes, runs a statistical test (e.g., a t-test, chi-square) and explains the interpretation of the results. I then asked him clarification questions. And finally, I get Stats 101.

My biggest takeaway to share with you was from the last case study, where we discussed a situation where one set of data looks better than another – but is not statistically significant. That is, a non-statistician would have said Option A is better than B. Whereas it isn't. The next step is to expand the test. As you expand the test, the truth of A being better than B, or not, will become more evident. That is, start small and low cost and expend more effort only as needed.

As you may not have access to the introduction of these case studies if you are not attending Risk and Cyber Week, feel free to get in touch for a little more explanation.

Stay safe and adapt – with better measurement!

Cheers
Bryan

# Control Geeks Not Freaks
27 July 2021

Process control has a very specific meaning in the chemical industry. It refers to the system used for controlling a chemical plant. All the various instruments on pumps, vessels, reactors, heat exchangers and the like feed into the control room where the operators monitor screens, react to alarms and manipulate the system to maximise output. If you have air conditioning, that little wall pad showing the temperature, is like the screens in the control room. There is a system controlling the temperature in your house.

The reason I raise this is because of information <u>Lyall Bear</u>, one of my readers, sent me in response to my invitation to my roundtable discussion next week on the future of risk frameworks. As I mentioned last week, I am uncertain as to what may be discovered, however, what I do know is that the topic is of interest. The seats filled fast, and I am now fielding enquiries from those who won't be in the room, wishing to hear about the results of the discussion. Something I will do, once I know what is to be shared!

Back to process control. In the information Lyall sent, which is from his research into effective business strategy implementation, was a diagram headed "Process control may be one of the most operational of tasks, but it can

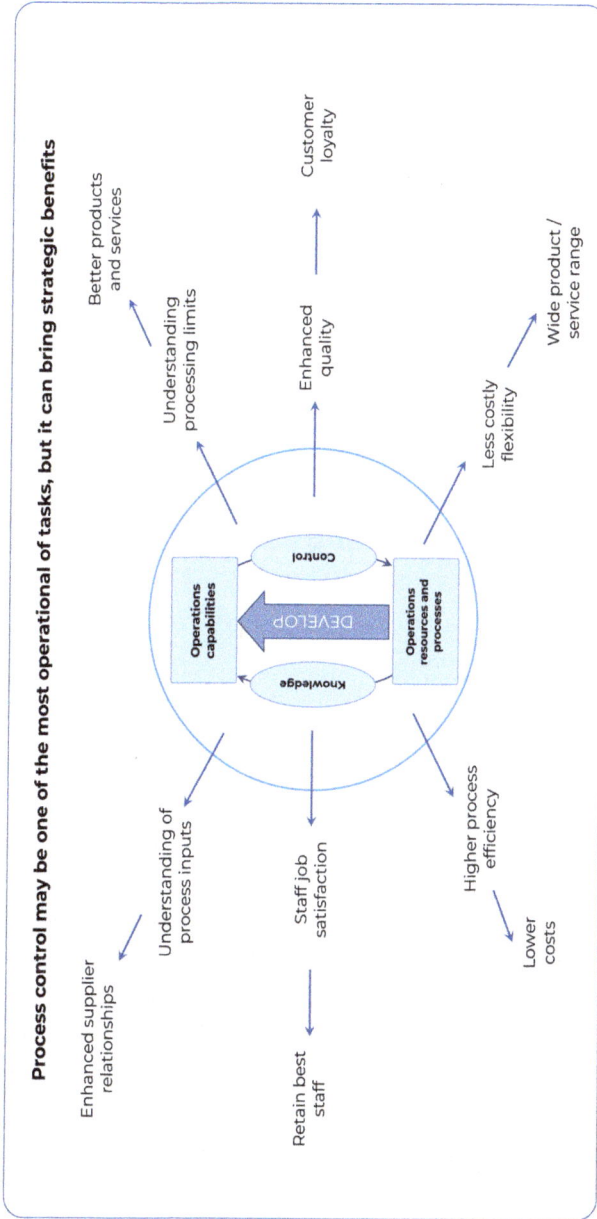

**Process control may be one of the most operational of tasks, but it can bring strategic benefits**

Figure 9: Benefits of Good Controls

Source: *"Essentials of Strategic Management: Effective Formulation and Execution of Strategy"* authored by Thomas Wunder in 2016

bring strategic benefits." (Refer previous page.) The statement was used in relation to any type of operation, not a chemical plant. This got me thinking about good versus bad control. Geeks versus freaks.

There is no doubt that in the case of a chemical or other type of manufacturing facility, good process control results in quality outcomes. This type of control is the domain of the best control geeks.

On the other hand, as I wrote about in Chapter 4: Agents of Complexity in my book *Risky Business: How Successful Organisations Embrace Uncertainty,* an organisation as a whole is a complex system and by definition can't be controlled. Any attempt to do so is doomed to failure. Hence the term 'control freak' being frequently used today.

The question you should be asking time and time again is: "What elements of this dynamic, complex process should I control and which should I just nudge and react to?" The former is the domain of the control geek. The latter, you must keep the control freak away from, if you want more agility in your organisation.

Thanks Lyall, based on the depth of your research, your clients are in safe hands with you.

Stay safe!

Cheers
Bryan

# INDUSTRY DISRUPTION

# Attack the Uncertainty of Disruption

24 January 2020

There is an adage that attack is the best form of defence. I'm very sure it applies when it comes to disruption.

Last blog (see my blog 'Does it Disturb or Excite You?') I asked if disruption disturbs or excites you and your colleagues. I also gave you some ammunition so you could scare your colleagues into action if that is what it takes to get their attention. And I promised to give you something, so you are not seen simply as the bearer of bad news. That something is that attack is the best form of defence. That thinking like a disrupter will mean you can make sense of the potential disruption happening or about to happen in your industry.

Whenever I am approached to help executives think about the risk posed by disruption, I work with friend and colleague Paul Broadfoot who is a disruption strategy specialist.

Together we provide the yin and yang for attacking disruption. We help you look at the risk and opportunity it presents by shifting mindsets from thinking like a traditional organisation to thinking like disrupters. We use Paul's methodologies for identifying disruptive strategies and then apply the risk process to identify the scale of the risk or opportunity.

Makes sense doesn't it? It's simply a variation of the process I preach in my <u>influencing program</u>. Normally it is stand in the shoes of those you want to influence and paint them a picture of a positive future. Instead it is stand in the shoes of disrupters and paint yourselves a positive picture of the world ahead. Simples!

Cheers
Bryan

*You want to be
the best in your
industry. The leader.
The disrupter.*

# Develop Disruptive Capability
3 February 2020

You want to be the best in your industry. The leader. The disrupter. Maybe you just want to think like a disrupter so you can understand the risk industry disruption poses to your organisation. No matter the reason, there is a question of capability.

You see, thinking like a disrupter is a mindset. And for traditional organisations it requires a mindset shift. To get you thinking, I recommend you watch this video or read the transcript.

Innovation is not enough. It's a blog by my colleague Paul Broadfoot who is a disruption strategy expert. In it he explains the difference between innovation and disruption. The contrast is stark.

Once you have watched the video or read the transcript check out this infographic about autonomous car connections. The message is clear – traditional organisations like the big car brands are partnering with disrupters and they are actively looking to disrupt themselves. This goes beyond innovation. They are developing approaches that include a reduction in vehicle ownership through shared ownership. They are developing mobile cinema platforms that also act as transportation. And they are developing technology that will wipe out hundreds of billions of dollars in investment in combustion engine technology. Of course, if they don't do it someone else will.

In the finance sector with things like blockchain and a massive assault on the way we all make payments <u>there are literally thousands of start-ups.</u> The progressive industry players are keeping a close eye on things. They are maintaining a presence in "fintech hubs" where start-ups come together to support each other and be supported.

Bankers know how to make money. They keep a very close eye on where the money will be, and they act. What about you? Do you know what is in play in your industry? Do you have the capability to even know where to look?

Develop disruptive capability. It starts with a shift in mindset.

Cheers
Bryan

# They're Mad as Hatters

10 February 2020

To you and me the disrupters are as mad as the Mad Hatter from Alice in Wonderland. And you could be led to believe we all live in Wonderland. Not true. Only some of them are. Then there are the ones that large smart investors back.

A couple of years back I went to an evening seminar to observe a fireside chat between the COO of start-up Finder, Jeremy Cabral and his friend Willix Halim, COO of Bukalapak. Bukalapak is an Indonesian tech unicorn (a unicorn is a privately held company with a valuation over $1 billion).

Bukalapak was one of Indonesia's largest e-commerce marketplaces. Halim described it as the Amazon app for Indonesia. You could buy a bus ticket or access finance on it. They were working to get more and more and more options onto it.

Halim also explained this was a critical tech start-up play. There were four contenders and one would become the Amazon of Indonesia, if not a large chunk of Asia. Much was at stake.

Then he mentioned that he was due to stay in Australia a few more days. However, he had heard that day that one of their main start-up competitors had announced they had just raised another US$30M in funding. He said he was heading home in the morning, to help raise that and then some.

There was no stress. No sense of a risk of failure. Equally there was no "pomp and circumstance". It was just what was needed to be done. What *would* be done.

I thought to myself, while it sounds like he is mad as a hatter, he simply lives in a different world. He and his colleagues think differently. And with the backing of companies like Alibaba Group Holdings through its Ant Financial Services Group and the Singaporean sovereign wealth fund GIC, you know the game is a serious one. One where there will be one big winner and many, many losers.

If you are now thinking you want to investigate disruption and the risk and opportunity it presents to your organisation, head to my blogs recorded on my website and check out my last few blogs on disruption. I think there are some very good tips for you to consider following.

Cheers
Bryan

# From Fear to Understood
## 17 February 2020

According to passiton.com and brainyquote.com (see I've done my research, the internet never lies, right?) Marie Curie said, "Nothing in life is to be feared; it is only to be understood."

For those of you who are not right up on Curie, she was a scientist who discovered the chemical element now on the periodic table called polodium (named after her native Poland) as well as radium from which we get the word radiation. Curie was a wonderful scientist who was awarded the Nobel Prize in Physics in 1903 and in Chemistry in 1911.

Her words about abandoning fear and seeking understanding are very true and not so true. First the untrue. Curie and her husband did not understand the risks they were taking when they were working with polodium and radium. They did not feel well at times and worked with hands that became red-raw from handling radioactive material. They suffered from what we now know is radiation sickness. Curie died after her husband in her sixties. Neither lived a particularly long life.

On the other hand, when it comes to something like industry disruption she was so very right. You and I should not fear it, we should look to understand it.

Look for early disrupters in the form of start-ups or new initiatives of competitors. Then go a step further and work out how you might disrupt your own industry. From there you have choices. Some may be tougher than others. However, at least they won't be forced on you.

Have I caught your interest in disruption? I hope so. Check out my last few blogs on disruption. I think there are some very good tips for you to consider following.

Cheers
Bryan

# LEADERSHIP

# The 4Cs of Decision Categorisation

17 March 2020

Categorising beyond Type 1 and Type 2 decisions that I wrote about in my last blog 'The key to being FaB-er' can help decision makers. And right now, decision makers across the world can do with all the help they can get given the recently declared pandemic.

The four Cs are Core, Complicated, Complex and Chaotic. The person behind this type of thinking is David Snowden and his Cynefin Framework shown alongside. The only difference is the category I call Core, he calls Obvious. As in decisions for which the answer should be obvious. In Snowden's model he explains that Core decisions need rigid constraints, Complicated decisions need governing constraints, Complex decisions need enabling constraints and in a Chaotic environment, there are no constraints. Anything goes.

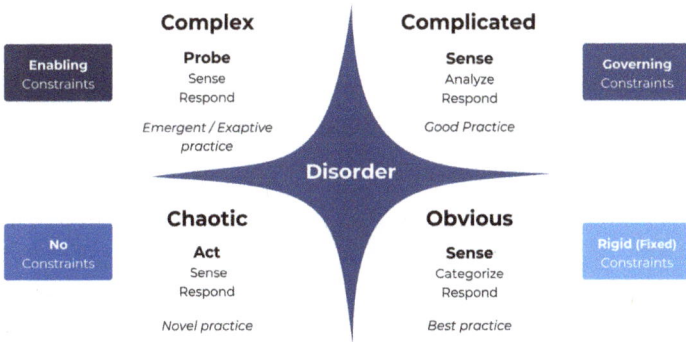

Figure 10: Cynefin Framework

Source: https://thecynefin.co/about-us/about-cynefin-framework/

It is the border between Complex and Chaotic I want to explore given the current environment. I think we can safely say that decision making around how to respond to the pandemic has gone beyond complicated. But is it chaotic or just complex?

Snowden makes two suggestions that help us understand if decision makers are operating in chaos or complexity and what to do in response. First, he says if you are facing chaos then introduce some constraints. For example: Closing borders to travel, introducing self-isolation. Second, he suggests that in a complex environment one of the ways we respond is through repurposing existing "assets". For example, repurposing empty hotels as temporary hospitals for COVID-19 patients or for quarantine purposes as is now planned in the UK.

My take. The decision-making environment for the authorities is bordering on the edge of complexity into chaos. However, the authorities are taking the right actions to introduce constraints and create ONLY a complex decision-making environment.

And to end off with a final note of compassion for those in the hot seats of power right now. Take this from US President John F Kennedy:

> "... the President bears the burden of the responsibility quite rightly. The advisers may move on to new advice."
> Washington Post December 18, 1962.

I wish the best for you and yours in these challenging times. Even more so, I wish the best for our authorities ... that they make the best decisions under the toughest of circumstances.

Cheers
Bryan

# It's Time to Slide Back Down the Curve a Bit
24 March 2020

S-curves are beautiful things. They are wonderful for helping to decide where we are and where we want to be. From what I have heard and observed this week, it is time to slide back down the curve a bit. Let me explain.

The figure below is the one I show to boards and executives when I describe for them the value of a strong approach to risk management. You move from feeling or being vulnerable and exposed, to adaptive, to resilient. And if you are very, very good, you become agile – making rapid decisions within envelopes of strong understanding of the organisation's appetite for taking certain risks.

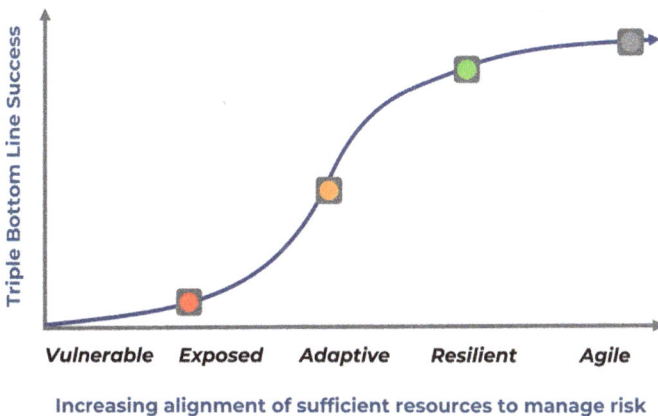

Figure 11: The Journey to Organisational Agility

An increasing number of organisations I work with these days are operating higher on the curve than ever before and are working with me in pursuit of greater resilience or to achieve agility. The problem is that the threat posed by COVID-19 is testing their agility, and for many, their resilience. I'm going to say to you that it is not just OK to slide back the curve a little. It is essential. Why? Let me tell you.

One of my good mates, let's call him Cam, highlighted an article for me this week that was published in Harvard Business Review in the midst of the GFC <u>Leadership in a (Permanent) Crisis</u>. The article was a timely reminder about the need for organisations to adopt Adaptive Leadership. That is, to slide back down the curve and operate in that place where you built your organisation's resilience in the first place. In our new reality, what it takes to be resilient and agile is being recreated before our very eyes.

While others have written extensively on <u>Adaptive Leadership</u>, let me give you my top tips to follow:

1. Act like a scientist and *experiment*. It's the best way to identify what will work and what won't.
2. Be *courageous* and be prepared to kill off sacred cows.
3. Rely on others and *devolve* decision making authority to them as you cannot do this on your own.

Feel free to share with someone if you think this will be helpful for them right now. It is definitely the time to be helping others.

Stay safe.

Cheers
Bryan

# Experiment to Stretch Your Teams
### 30 March 2020

It is wonderous how adaptive we are and I as I wrote last week (see my blog 'It's time to slide back down the curve a bit'), Adaptive Leadership is key right now. Top of the list of my tips for exercising Adaptive Leadership is to experiment. Now I know we are all experimenting at the moment, one way or another, just to get by. However, with our incredible ability to adapt, you and your teams are adjusting at a pace that many will be surprised by. So, now that much of the mad scramble to adjust to new ways of working has happened, let's start thinking about experimenting to stretch you and your teams.

There are three key components to experimentation:

- Drivers – The goal(s) you are seeking.
- Design – The well-established principles of sound experimentation.
- Decision – The interpretation of the results and the action you take.

First is drivers. The purpose of your experimentation will naturally be driven by your challenges right now. You have challenges of ensuring your teams are safe and well,

*The purest and most successful form of experimentation is the scientific method. It maximises the utility of the experiment by minimising the chance the results are misleading.*

that they are re-planning their delivery of your strategy and that they are productive. Whether it is all of these or just one of them, get very clear on the purpose of your experimentation. Then get moving, get productive and set up your online collaboration for the experiment. Here are some tips from my friend, colleague and productivity expert Dermot Crowley <u>on working with online tools in the current environment.</u> If you and your team are not skilled up on how to run reliable experiments, there are some great online resources such as <u>Explorable</u> and <u>Dummies</u>.

Second is design. The purest and most successful form of experimentation is the scientific method. It maximises the utility of the experiment by minimising the chance the results are misleading. It requires some effort, however, these are times to lean in, not shy away.

Finally there is decision. For this, I can't go past my <u>MCI Decision Model</u> (see my blog <u>'Working with our tendency for</u> impulsiveness') to help you here. M is for *motivation,* C is for *clarification* and I is for *implementation.* In short. Don't go straight to implementation. Clarify the approach you are planning. What are the obstacles to overcome and what are the potential unintended consequences? And finally, just check that the motivation is right. Are you answering the right question? If you have done a fine job with step one, confirming the drivers that determines the purpose of your experimentation, you should be able to answer yes to this question. For more information on the MCI Decision Model, you can access a short paper here.

Stay safe.

Cheers
Bryan

# Courage Sprouts Risk and Opportunity
## 7 April 2020

Being courageous with your decision making is key to Adaptive Leadership which I have been writing about for the last couple of weeks. Easy to say, yet you and I both know that courageous decisions are full of risk and opportunity. Will it work? What will it cost me? What unforeseen problems am I creating? Yet, the need requires the risk, or the opportunity is simply too significant to pass up.

Take the manufacturers turning to supply plastic face masks with 3D printers or the ones now producing much needed medical equipment. They are practicing Adaptive Leadership, putting trust in their people to come up with the answers through experimentation and hard work.

The risk is they may fail, making a potentially bad situation worse. The opportunity is significant. They can help save lives, and they may save their business along with countless jobs.

Courage is easy to see when people like members of our defence force or emergency services put their lives on the line for us. Fortunately, they are trained to make courageous decisions in a fast paced and often chaotic environment. They are given a simple set of rules based on years and years of experience.

For the rest of us, operating in unchartered waters, we don't have a set of tried and tested rules. So, let me share with you these three tips on courageous decision making:

**Conversations** – You must have the difficult conversations now. Don't put them off. Whether they be about pay cuts for staff or about managers giving up control.

**Voices** – You must listen to the voices from outside your trusted inner circle. Your inner circle has never been through something quite like this. They may not have the right answers. Listen to the dissenters and work out how you can experiment and test their views against the views of your inner circle.

**Risks** – You must take calculated risks. The same rules apply as always. You never bite off more than you can chew, unless you have no other choice. And a bad risk assessment is worse than no risk assessment as our intuitive judgement is better. So do your risk assessment with the right people, with the best available information and take the time to get it right.

Stay safe and move quickly.

Cheers
Bryan

# Devolve Decision Making
## 9 April 2020

Devolving decision making is another key element of Adaptive Leadership. At its core, devolved decision making is about recognising that you and your trusted inner circle of advisers don't have all the answers and so you must trust your people to come up with the answers.

To coin a phrase from Heifetz et al, authors of *The Practice of Adaptive Leadership*, it's about "micro adaptation". It's lots of people adapting lots of ways and often. This needs to occur at the level of the individual, team and business unit level.

You also need to acknowledge the independence of your people in their homes right now. And allow them that independence and give them the trust to do the right thing, while they are home schooling, caring for the elderly or disabled or dealing with the troubles that will arise from home isolation with others.

While you are giving your teams their independence, it is vitally important that you also consider the interdependence that exists across your organisation. While an individual or a team or business unit may be given the authority to experiment and make decisions, who do they need to communicate that decision to? Who might be affected? Who could benefit if only they knew?

This leads on nicely to the three questions of Adaptive Leadership:

1. What?
2. Who?
3. When?

The first question is: "What are the things we need to be courageous about and experiment on? – What are the sacred cows we are going to challenge?" Whatever you think was a line you couldn't cross before ... rethink the need for it or rethink how you can cross the line without any unwanted collateral damage.

The next question is: "Who are you going to devolve responsibility to in terms of experimentation?" Team leaders, individuals?

And lastly: "When?" When are you going to allow your teams to be courageous in their own right and do the experiments that you know can make a difference in these tough times?

Stay safe and adapt – quickly.

Cheers
Bryan

# Tooling for Adaptive Leadership
20 April 2020

My blog a few weeks back encouraging you to <u>slide back down the maturity curve</u> and grasp <u>Adaptive Leadership</u> with both hands, has lead me to consider the analysis tools we have available and which would be most useful when looking to be adaptive.

There are a bunch of tools I use regularly. They include Stakeholder Analysis, PESTLE Analysis, Porter's Industry Five Forces, Unique Value Proposition, Value Chain Analysis and my very own Capability Analysis (<u>templates for most of these are available with examples here</u>). These coupled with risk analysis techniques are very effective for improving decision making. And you should keep on using them now as much as ever.

However, there is one tool that I use that has proven invaluable. And that is Scenario Analysis. Over recent weeks I have had the opportunity to assist a range of clients by facilitating workshops to help them work through various scenarios of where their business could be over the next 1, 3, 6 and 12 months. Helping them work through good, bad and very bad scenarios, and what the impact could be on their staff, customers, finances and a range of other elements of their business.

No one can predict the future, but we can imagine it.

While it would have been extremely difficult to imagine our upturned world sitting in our lounge rooms a few months ago, many aspects of it were not impossible to predict. It is because of our ability to imagine that epidemiologists warned us of global pandemics (and picked up by the <u>World Economic Forum as one of the world's top ten risks in 2020 in terms of impact</u>). It is why there was a national stockpile of much needed medical equipment. The irony is that the antivirals don't work on COVID-19 but we already knew that from SARS.

Scenario analysis is a tool that requires us to imagine a range of scenarios in the future which leads us to make decisions today in preparation for as many variants of the future as your imagination uncovers.

In my recent world, scenario analysis has won hands down when it comes to the most important tool in my tool kit. If you have not used it in a structured manner, I encourage you to do so. It is much more effective than a group of leaders talking and surmising about what might or might not be.

Stay safe and adapt – quickly.

Cheers
Bryan

*Listening is important in any conversation. However, listening to the voices that you don't normally hear from is critical at this time.*

# Adaptive Leadership Through Listening
28 April 2020

Listening is important in any conversation. However, listening to the voices that you don't normally hear from is critical at this time. Those from outside your normal circle of trusted advisers.

I run a <u>mentoring group</u> once a month. At my most recent one I presented my views on Adaptive Leadership which gave a lens to look through to view how our organisations are responding to the current crisis. A common theme that came through strongly was that the best leaders were most definitely communicating broadly. And not just communicating with updates, they were facilitating two-way communication. And of-course, broad, two-way communication allows you to listen to those outside your inner circle. A core attribute of Adaptive Leadership. Here are a couple of examples:

## Hospitals

One of the members of my group, who is a senior leader in a hospital environment, shared a video that had been prepared for all staff. It was led by the CEO followed by a star-studded cast of senior leaders from the hospital. Who were they? They were leaders who were clinicians, human resources, facilities management and from several other core operational areas. What were they doing? They were answering questions from staff that had been sent in. Everything from advice on the virus and PPE supplies to issues of leave and screening of staff. By asking for their questions the leadership group were hearing their concerns.

## Insurance

Another member of the group from an insurance company described how quickly and easily his organisation had adjusted to remote working. The organisation already had a significant level of devolved decision making, another critical element of Adaptive Leadership, but it was the approach of the senior leaders with two-way communication that was so impressive. Every team member received a phone call from a senior leader each week through the first month of working from home. Every team member. Every week. And each leader did plenty of listening.

While not discussed explicitly, I am sure that what was being heard was being reflected on in senior management meetings. At least weekly.

I know many of us have a lot on our plates. Everything seems to be taking a little longer, even if we are moving forward. However, prioritising reaching out further to staff (than you normally would) is something you are likely to find highly rewarding. Especially if you listen!

Stay safe and adapt – quickly.

Cheers
Bryan

# Examples of Adaptive Leadership

5 May 2020

Given my focus on Adaptive Leadership in my blogs over the past six weeks, when one of my clients shared this with me recently, I just had to share it more widely. It is a wonderful example of Adaptive Leadership. In this case, in the aged care sector.

To remind you, the three attributes I see at the core of Adaptive Leadership are:

- Being courageous
- Proactively Experimenting
- Devolving Decision Making

In this interview on Skynews, Stephen Judd, CEO of HammondCare explains to host, Kieran Gilbert, how HammondCare has tried to get the balance right in their aged care facilities. As he commenced his explanation, Judd was quick to point out that no aged care provider deserves criticism for their response when compared to any other provider as each is operating with a different set of circumstances.

Irrespective, as you can imagine, the easiest way to keep aged residents safe and to avoid criticism is to lockdown facilities to visitors and only allow staff and necessary contractors. HammondCare took a different approach.

They "actively experimented" via survey of those in their care and via consultation with their representative groups. They found overwhelming support for the continuation of visits. Next, they empowered their teams to make each facility as safe as practically possible within the legal requirements set by the Federal Government. Via a little thoughtful creativity, they introduced the concept of a concierge. Their job at each facility is to politely screen every visitor, staff member or contractor with questions and temperature checks. And they applied and reinforced all the rules around social distancing during visits.

At the time of the interview, HammondCare did not have any cases of COVID-19 in any of their facilities. But even if they did, they managed the risk with eyes-wide-open having had the conversation with their most important stakeholders. The aged residents under their care.

Stay safe and adapt – quickly.

Cheers
Bryan

# Diagnosis Precedes Action in Leadership
## 2 June 2020

Whether you are planning to lead on tackling a problem in your organisation or an opportunity to improve your own leadership, diagnosis comes first. A mechanic should not start stripping the engine before conducting some diagnostics. Nor should you buy a personal development book without asking yourself what type of book might serve you best.

In *The Practice of Adaptive Leadership*, Heifetz et al makes the point very clearly that there are two core processes to leadership. Diagnosis and action. And that diagnosis precedes action. They present a 2x2 matrix showing the four different positions you could be taking in your leadership role. I have gone one step further and named the quadrants with the key action you should be undertaking in each. See Figure 12.

And in reading this work, I was reminded of my own self diagnosing experience when I was last an employee in a large corporate (gulp ... some 19 years ago!) I had the opportunity to be involved in a leadership development program. It was an excellent program and we had some of the best leadership coaches, facilitators and trainers in the business.

I remember one poignant moment early in the program that brought home to me that I was in a leadership DEVELOPMENT program, and not a program to reward my exceptional leadership.

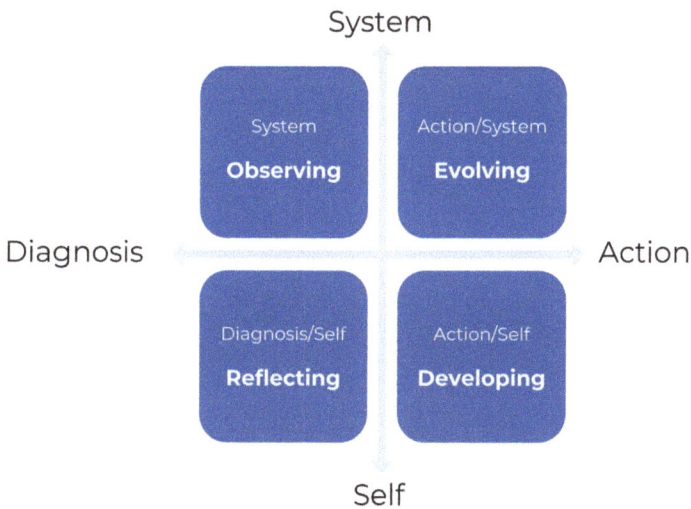

Figure 12: The Diagnosis Matrix

We were split into teams and I was picked by the team as team leader. We also had to pick a deputy leader. I quickly nominated a person in the team who I liked and had developed some respect for. There was immediate rebellion in the team. While they had elected me their leader, they had not elected me as universal decision maker on all things affecting the team.

The learning curve had begun. I was in a Leadership

DEVELOPMENT Program and the diagnosis had started!

Stay safe and adapt – quickly.

Cheers
Bryan

# Strategising with So Much Uncertainty

9 June 2020

Uncertainty? What uncertainty? The one thing that is certain is that there will always be uncertainty!

I've been thinking more deeply recently about the problems leaders like you are potentially dealing with. One of the most pressing problems falls on the demand side of your business. Some customers may have gone out of business or completely shut down for now. Others are hurting badly and cutting costs any way they can. While many others are tightening purse strings even though they have not been too badly impacted as yet. Why? Uncertainty as to what is coming next. Even your customers who are doing really well right now have uncertainty as to how long the good times will continue to roll.

Having been immersed in this thinking last week, I was speaking to a friend who is the CFO of a large Australian company in the construction supply chain. He asked how I was doing through COVID. One thing I commented on, was that the extra time not travelling had allowed me (perhaps given me the energy) to do some really good, deeper work.

He commented he was envious of me having time for

deep thinking. "Here in big corporate we are reacting and scenario planning and trying to work out how to deliver on our strategy with all the uncertainty of what might be or not be over the coming months." I said to him "Adaptive Leadership! That is what I have been deep thinking about these past couple of months. The leadership style best suited to navigating our way through the coming months. Let me send you a paper on it."

If you have not already done so, you can get my paper on Adaptive Leadership here.

Stay safe and adapt – quickly.

Cheers
Bryan

# Rewarding Risk

24 May 2022

Short on time? Go to the end to find out what "rewarding risk" is all about.

I'm blogging on accountability at the top for risk. Last week I led off with the story of Val King and her experience of risk appetite (see my blog 'Embedding Accountability') being an avenue to increase accountability for risk at all levels of the organisation.

Have you asked yourself why people don't take accountability for the more formal management of risk our risk frameworks demand? In particular, senior leaders?

In my experience, a lack of accountability is not a conscious choice by a leader. It is a circumstance of something else. For example:

- Buy-in – They have not been "sold" on why they should pay attention to and engage with the requirements of the framework.
- Engagement – Despite hearing the why, they won't buy-in because they feel the requirements were thrust upon them. "Another bloody thing to do!"

- Clarity – A lack of understanding of what is practically required of them.
- Resources – They don't have the headspace. They are so busy keeping balls in the air, they are tackling the now rather than what might be.

Or it could be that they have legitimately engaged with the requirements of the risk framework and been left underwhelmed. They have not felt sufficient reward for their efforts. If you saw effort and then the lack of accountability, you will need to look at the "risk versus reward" equation for leaders and increase the reward. More on that to come. 😀

Stay safe!

Cheers
Bryan

# Organisation Think
## 16 February 2021

No doubt you have heard of *groupthink*, how the desire to conform – so a group remains of like-mind – can lead to poor decisions. There is another phenomenon at play that I call *organisation think*, through which the culture of an organisation influences HOW a decision is implemented.

The effect of organisational culture on decision making was powerfully driven home for me by reading *Essence of Decision: Explaining the Cuban Missile Crisis* (2nd Edition) by Graham Allison and Philip Zelikow. In short, leaders make decisions and staff implement them, which requires them to interpret meaning and to identify means of achieving perceived goals.

In the case of the Cuban missile crisis, Khruschchev failed to account for organisation think. The Soviet mission was ostensibly a secret operation. The US was not supposed to know. But when the Soviets built missile bases in Cuba they did not camouflage them from the air. Why?

Allison and Zelikow suggest it was because the Soviet forces responsible implemented as they had always implemented — according to the manual. The decision had been made not to camouflage bases in the Soviet Union to aid speed of deployment. That is, agility was chosen over secrecy. When it came to the deployment in Cuba, the message did not get through that this deployment was to be different. And when the skies cleared sufficiently, a U2 spy plane was able to get the evidence needed that would ultimately put Khruschchev on the back foot causing him to order a withdrawal of the missile bases.

The lesson for senior leaders in organisations is the importance of understanding organisational culture when making a decision in order to understand how a decision will be interpreted and whether it requires cultural change. If the need for change is not identified and managed, the initiative is likely to fail or at least be heavily impaired.

I explore this concept of organisation think in my new book *Risky Business: How Successful Organisations Embrace Uncertainty*.

Stay safe.

Cheers
Bryan

*If the need for change
is not identified
and managed, the
initiative is likely
to fail or at least be
heavily impaired.*

# Pathways to Success
8 June 2021

Since February I have been sending you messages from my book *Risky Business: How Successful Organisations Embrace Uncertainty.* In the penultimate chapter of the book, Chapter 11: The Pathways to Success, I describe the journey of a risk practitioner who sees much work to do in an organisation near void of risk-based decision making.

The key pathways to success are through educating leaders on the benefits of risk-based decision making while simultaneously cultivating a culture that truly reflects the values of the organisation. Eventually you move from a role requiring plenty of educating and cultivating to a point where you are "leading alongside". Like an adult friend advising on a decision.

You have truly succeeded when business leaders work with you to ensure they overcome their unconscious biases and are making decisions in full consideration of organisational values.

To read more you can download Chapter 11: Pathways to Success. Better still, buy my book and gain access to free resources that are there to help organisations perform better, faster! Stay safe!

Cheers
Bryan

# Implementing Through Doom and Gloom

24 August 2021

Four years ago I wrote about <u>Implementing in the Dark</u>. In it I pointed out that the scorecard for executive teams when it comes to major, strategic decisions is pretty poor. With fail rates estimated between 40 and 50%.

I went on to say that much of it can be explained because leaders were implementing in the dark. That is, leaders are sometimes blissfully unaware of how their decisions will be implemented in practice by staff in their organisation. For all major decisions there are assumptions inherently made about how staff will act in implementation of the decision. And if those assumptions do not align perfectly to organisational culture, they are misinformed.

In today's world even the most intuitive leadership team is at risk of this phenomenon. Because so much is being implemented with a feeling of doom and gloom. Whether in lockdown or not, the uncertainty of the next 12 months is telling on people's minds. Playing cruel tricks on every staff member.

Four years ago I wrote: "If a leader does not properly understand these nuances (of organisational culture), they are working in the dark and the intent of their decision is not likely to be realised."

Today leadership teams need to double down to understand how culture may have changed or is changing week to week.

Stay safe!

Cheers
Bryan

# Reactivity Leads to Captivity
12 October 2021

Taking a reactive approach to risk management means we are captive to limited thinking.

This blog was prompted by a question from a participant in the webinar I ran with Camms Group last month on Risk Reporting: How to Provide Summary in Detail. The question was: "Is risk management reactive or proactive? Risk assessment being about what happened rather than what might happen in the next quarter or next 6 months."

When I run the RMIA's Enterprise Risk Management course or my Mastering Risk Workshop Facilitation course I run an activity to make sure participants understand the true purpose of risk assessment (Hint: It's not to collect a bunch of risks). It's to ask interesting questions to help people unleash their minds from inherent beliefs and our penchant to believe our plan will work. Because it is our plan after all.

At the same time as pondering this issue I sent this article, How to Mine Synthetic Data: Pros and Cons of a Shiny New Tool for Risk Managers, to my colleague Dr Andrew Pratley to get his views on it. He replied with comments around the uncertainty of "black boxes" built on these approaches, ending with:

"I think the most important point she made was to note that usually big changes are negative and no model will predict this the first time it happens. People need to think about more casual factors than torturing the historical data for answers that don't exist."

Therein lies a perfect example of the need to unlock our captive thinking. The trick is identifying how in-depth to go. The more critical the outcome sought, the deeper you should dig into your mind and the minds of others.

Stay safe!

Cheers
Bryan

*The more critical
the outcome sought,
the deeper you
should dig into
your mind and the
minds of others.*

# Selling Resilience
19 October 2021

This week I'm sharing my paper 'Selling Resilience' with you that I wrote for those who understand the benefits of building resilience to enshrine organisational value and know that convincing the unenlightened is often hard to do. You see some people making decisions for short-term gain while riding their luck because it is the easier choice. Others you see being forced into decision making based on short-term time horizons because of politics or the views of analysts or the short-sightedness of customers.

You know that an organisation's responsibility to its stakeholders is to enshrine hard earned organisational value, not to leave the organisation so exposed it may be irrevocably damaged. You know that enshrining value takes foresight, resources and the courage of commitment. You also know that it requires the commitment of many stakeholders, not just the risk department or the board or the CEO. You know you need to bring a raft of internal and external stakeholders along with you, otherwise your plans for resilience fail or at best you achieve piecemeal success.

My aim with this paper is to provide you with a blueprint for engaging the unenlightened, to give you the tools to help them understand their options and to guide them to enshrine the hard- earned value in your organisation. For the full paper click <u>here</u>.

Enjoy! And as always let me know your thoughts on this. I'd love to hear what you are thinking about risk and organisational resilience.

Cheers
Bryan

# Reactivity
1 March 2022

I very much enjoyed General Stanley McChrystal's _Team of Teams._ I'll definitely draw on his observations as I get fully stuck into writing my next book _Team Think – How Teams Make Great Decisions._

Here is a great summary article in Chief Executive about Gen. McChrystal's Risk Immune System analogy he espouses in his latest book _Risk: A User's Guide._ The analogy of HIV/AIDS not being the cause of death of HIV/AIDS sufferers. They die from other causes once their defences are compromised. He explains that organisations don't fail from a risk event, they fail by not reacting appropriately to the event.

McChrystal goes onto explain ten "risk control factors" from communication and structure to leadership and diversity. However, perhaps most important is Adaptability. It is the essence of Change Management which is a constant challenge for risk professionals as you grow the maturity of your organisation in managing risk.

In early 2020 I wrote extensively on Adaptive Leadership, a term coined by Ronald Heifetz, Alexander Grashow and Marty Linsky in their Harvard Business Review article published in the midst of the GFC in 2009 titled _Leadership in a (Permanent) Crisis_. I published my take

*Yes you need to be courageous. Sometimes you need to fight for a seat at the table. Yes you need to experiment to find out what works, what creates behavioural change.*

on this style of leadership in which I espoused leaders to pursue:

1. Being Courageous
2. Proactive Experimentation
3. Devolved Decision Making

Almost the exact same applies for you as a risk professional creating change in your organisation to grow maturity. Yes you need to be courageous. Sometimes you need to fight for a seat at the table. Yes you need to experiment to find out what works, what creates behavioural change. But my spin on the last one is that you need to pursue "Involved Decision Making". That is, decisions by leaders that involve you or at least involve an appropriate level of discussion about risk.

Stay safe and make change.

Cheers
Bryan

# Surprise Surprise!

12 July 2022

I was working with a CEO recently who had been in the job for about a year. When they started, they found – surprise, surprise – all was not as it was made out to be. It was a very difficult environment. The challenges were more than challenges, they were wicked problems. And the road ahead a very, very rocky one.

It got me thinking about you and what you might want to consider before you accept a CRO, or other senior, job offer in risk. Here are my top three tips:

1. ***Due Diligence:*** Is this organisation right for you? What is the organisation's mission, vision and, most importantly, values? Nice start. Do they live their values? Head over to social media and see what you can find. Then to the job search companies like Seek and Glassdoor to check out company reviews. Better still, talk to someone who works there if you can.

   What about their management of risk? Can you check out company performance over the last five years? Publicly listed and public sector organisations will have the most information available. Most not-for-profits publish pretty detailed annual reports that you can put a discerning eye over, however, in Australia where I am based, the Australian Charities and Not for Profits Commission (ACNC) has a company overview for all registered charities. Each overview has a History page which will include any enforcement action by the ACNC.

Then there are all the other regulators of industries that public and private for-profit organisations operate in e.g. finance sector, aged care, food, tertiary education. Each of these regulators can be a source of information about enforcement actions or other issues you may find concerning.

Please, don't do your due diligence through rose coloured glasses because you want the job that badly! Maybe get a close confidant to give an opinion on what you find. However, the reason they may be seeking your skills is because they truly want to turn around their culture and/or performance, which leads on to the next two tips.

2. *Authority:* What are your reporting lines and your decision-making authority? Do they reflect an organisation that is serious about managing risk for success rather than managing risk to meet compliance obligations? Ideally a CRO is on the executive team. When it comes to access to board and committees of the board, this depends on the risk management model in place or desired by the

organisation. In the Three Lines Model favoured by regulators, it is very clear that the CRO must have direct access to the board and board committees. In a tri-partite model of risk management (see my blog 'Design Success – Kill TLM and Adopt T-PM') where the CRO is adviser, as opposed to challenger, the approach would be to have standing agenda type items where the board or committees hear the CRO's views on future performance and advice on key decisions.

If the role you are looking at is reporting to a CRO or an executive on the leadership team who is the notional CRO, I would be trying to understand their level of understanding of what it takes to have a fantastic risk culture. And as you know, it starts with the executive team. It will be hard work if you have to constantly <u>fight to be heard</u> by the executive and board.

3. **Budget:** The proof is in the pudding. Ensure you have your own budget, and it is sufficient for the resources you will need. Too many times I have worked with CROs that had to get approval from the Audit and Risk Committee to spend what I would consider a small amount of money in the scheme of things.

When negotiating budget, I hope you have quantification of risk on your mind. Many organisations have data, or could create data, for much more informed decision making about risk. Quantifying risk is easier when it is strictly about finances. However, it has been well proven by the likes of Doug Hubbard, author of _How to Measure Anything_, that much, much, much more can be done than is the case in many organisations.

Cheers
Bryan

# SCENARIO PLANNING

# Never Mistake Motion for Action
12 May 2020

"Never Mistake Motion for Action" is a quote attributed to novelist Ernest Hemingway. This is poignant in the current environment because motion *affects* results while action *effects* results. Said another way, if you create motion, something will happen. If you take action, you plan something to happen.

A few weeks ago I wrote about <u>tooling for Adaptive Leadership</u>. I was asking you to consider the analysis tools you have available to you to help you be adaptive through a time of great uncertainty. I listed many, but I homed in on one. Scenario Planning. A tool that requires us to imagine a range of scenarios in the future which leads us to make decisions today in preparation for a range of variants in the future.

Answer me this question. Have you and/or your executive team been discussing possible scenarios or have you been Scenario Planning. Discussing scenarios creates motion. You and others will most likely do something as a result of mulling over different scenarios. However, if you move from discussing to planning, you put yourself in the best place to manage whichever scenario plays out. Because you plan your actions with intent.

While you might find this a tad nuanced, the results can

be stark. It's why Hemingway's quote is so meaningful and can reflect the difference between saying "I'm so glad we did ..." versus "I wished we had ..."

Stay safe and adapt – quickly.

Cheers
Bryan

# Assumption Busting
## 19 May 2020

Laid out in front of you are a range of scenarios as to how the coming months might play out. You have already been shocked and surprised since our world got turned on its head. How many more surprises are coming your way? What might you do about them?

The answer is assumption busting. Identifying and clearly articulating the assumptions underlying each scenario and asking how you can test those assumptions to reduce uncertainty. Let me give you an example of how assumption busting works in practice.

Early in the COVID-19 crisis I reached out to some of my clients who I knew would be responding on behalf of all of us. Health, emergency services and the like. I offered to help with scenario planning. They took up my offer.

One of the key assumptions I worked with was, if Italy could get as bad as it had, so could Australia. A reasonable assumption given the amount of media commentary issuing similar warnings.

However, the message from Chief Medical Officer, Brendan Murphy, was different. Our testing regime would make the difference. So, I went looking for evidence. And sure enough, our rate of testing per head of population was way higher than most other countries. Even more importantly, our % of positive tests per 100 tests was way lower than other countries. We were near to 1% whereas other countries like the US and Canada were closer to 15%. Meaning, the virus had spread much further in those countries than it had in ours.

Testing assumptions is critical to any assessment. No more so than in highly uncertain times.

Remember, never ASSUME, as it may just make an ASS out of U and ME.

Stay safe and adapt – quickly.

Cheers
Bryan

# Design Think Your Way Out
26 May 2020

Some problems are seemingly intractable. One for you right now might be: "How do I plan for August when the current easing of social distancing and isolation restrictions may get reversed in a week, in a month or in the last week of July?"

One answer is to use Design Thinking, to work smart in addition to remaining agile. Design Thinking is a way of identifying new and innovative ideas. Sometimes to develop new products or services. And just as often to identify solutions to problems, especially intractable ones.

The five-stage process I use when facilitating Design Thinking for clients is the five-phase model of the Hasso-Plattner Institute of Design at Stanford University:

- Empathise – with stakeholders.
- Define – their needs, problems and insights you have about them.
- Ideate – challenge your assumptions to create innovative solutions.
- Prototype – to start creating solutions.
- Test – solutions.

Last week I asked you to test assumptions (see my

*Design Thinking is a way of identifying new and innovative ideas. Sometimes to develop new products or services. And just as often to identify solutions to problems, especially intractable ones.*

blog 'Assumption Busting') in relation to how various scenarios might play out over the coming months. The difference now in design thinking mode is that I'm asking you to test your assumptions about how your organisation can respond. That is, I am asking you to ideate, prototype and test your way to better ways of running your business so you can thrive under any scenario. The most successful organisations over the next six months will be the ones that work smart as well as being agile.

Want some examples? How about organisations such as boutique breweries manufacturing hand sanitiser. Schools working out how to teach online. Fitness centres becoming suppliers of gym equipment on short-term rental agreements. And bars and restaurants looking to design take-home experiences – cocktails, wine plus dishes that present well out of a plastic tub!

Over the past 10 weeks I have been writing about Adaptive Leadership. I have wrapped my thoughts up into a paper and it is my pleasure to share it with you Adaptive Leadership: Working smart while being agile.

Stay safe and adapt – quickly.

Cheers
Bryan

## ETU
30 November 2021

ETU or Expect the Unexpected has never been more apt a saying than over the past 21 months. And, with a wee few headlines (ha!) about Omicron to remind us as we start winding down for the calendar year and start planning our 2022 ... how should we plan?

A good question. I'll give you two answers based on recent personal experience.

The first answer has been with us forever, however, it was enshrined in the minds of millions through <u>Baden-Powell,</u> the founder of Scouts – Be Prepared!

Last weekend I was away with some mates staying in a hotel and the weather was forecast to be horrendous. I said to them that I was going to bring full wet weather gear so we could press on no matter the weather. I asked if anyone wanted a spare pair of rain pants I had, and there was a taker. As I went past my golf bag to the car, I decided to throw in my extra golf rain jacket and pants in case someone needed them.

There were only five of us on this trip, and the chance of one of them forgetting, was on the cards – but not two! And you guessed it, off we headed on Saturday morning to buy another set of rain jackets and pants. Fortunately for my mate, the sales were still on and he scored a bargain. 😊

This leads on to my second answer – just keep moving ahead regardless.

The previous weekend (yes, catching up for lost time) I travelled to Melbourne to play a weekend of golf organised by one of my mates who had been doing it hard in Melbourne's lockdowns. Organising it whilst scanning the horizon as to when the borders would open, helped keep him going during the last lockdown.

On the Wednesday before the weekend, he announces his double vaccinated son has COVID and he would need to isolate for 7 days as a close, double vaccinated, contact. What did we do? We pressed on, we kept in touch with him to help keep him going and he even subbed in his parents late one afternoon to have a drink with us. It was marvellous for them, us and my mate. We had just finished playing his golf course which he had been telling us a lot about in the lead up. He was feeling very chuffed.

And yes he caught COVID as well but everyone is fine. Just had to wait it out in isolation with cold-like symptoms for a few days.

To reiterate. Be prepared and keep moving ahead. We have proven we are good at adaptation and we adapt better the more prepared we are, so don't forget to do plenty of <u>scenario planning</u>.

Stay safe!

Cheers
Bryan

# Appetite Scenarios
7 December 2021

Over the last few months, I have been doing some non-risk work with a government agency. When I say non-risk work, they have engaged me not as a risk expert but as an expert in decision making. In part, because of my first book *DECIDE: How to Manage the Risk in your Decision Making,* and in part due to the new tools I have been developing as I research my new book *Team Think: How Teams Make Great Decisions.*

As you and I know, risk management is about improving decision making. Yet, it is not always the answer. In the case of this government agency, they had a range of teams making highly complex decisions under varying degrees of uncertainty. While risk comes into it, so too does the mechanics of routine team decision making.

What I have been helping them with is developing decision maps and identifying where decision support tools will enhance the accuracy, speed and consistency of decision making. And lo and behold, while risk assessment was the answer on occasion, most often it was non-risk tools like multi-criteria decision analysis (OK it is a risk tool but most people don't see it that way) that were needed.

To my pleasant surprise, risk came into it automatically

*Over the last few months, I have been doing some non-risk work with a government agency. When I say non-risk work, they have engaged me not as a risk expert but as an expert in decision making.*

for the teams I worked with in the form of appetite for risk. In particular, appetite for risk under various scenarios.

In the private sector, risk versus reward is often a much clearer picture than in government. Agency staff have the opinions of many, many more stakeholders to look to, to balance and always consider the views of the government of the day. Hence, some of the teams had already developed tools to help them identify the "sweet spot" or "least worst spot" for appetite for risk. These tools combined with a strong capability to develop and consider multiple scenarios quickly is the future for this agency.

Last week I wrote about the need for a focus on scenario planning for your plans for 2022. My message today, is to make sure you remember to have a very clear discussion about appetite for risk under each scenario. Don't assume. It is very likely to shift, sometimes a lot, from one scenario to another.

Stay safe!

Cheers
Bryan

## Risking Scenarios
14 December 2021

Recently I was discussing scenario planning with a small group of colleagues from the risk profession. I asked what scenario planning they or their organisation did. The answers were generally around dramatic changes that could happen in the next 12 months e.g. pandemic-related, China-related, regulation-post-royal-commission-related.

We soon agreed that this was just good risk management and was more scenario analysis than scenario planning. When I think scenario planning, I think 3-5 years unless you are the Department of Defence who must think 30 years as it takes so long to acquire some capabilities like submarines.

We then went on to discuss the role of the risk function in strategic planning. Hopefully the risk function gets included in the planning process, not just at the end to assess risk to the plan, as we have the tools and type of thinking that can ensure a quality strategic plan.

Take scenario planning as an example. For one, we should be promoting the development of a fairly wide range of scenarios for 1, 3 and 5 years out, to stimulate everyone's thinking. Great, but it is one thing to develop a range of scenarios, it is another thing to stop, think and get a good handle on the risks and opportunities each one poses. Estimating strategic consequence and likelihood is difficult enough for the next 12 months, let alone in 3 or 5 years.

Once of the answers I encourage for estimating highly uncertain scenarios is to crowd source answers from your staff. This technique is broadly outlined in this 8-minute video by Mariano Sigman and Dan Ariely. It involves asking small teams in your organisation to make estimates and then averaging them. On the one hand it seems a whole lot of effort. On the other hand, it is a great way to engage with staff on strategic direction.

Such an approach coupled with the design of lead indicators (KRIs if you like) that you can monitor over time will lead to better preparedness for a changing landscape and hence a more agile organisation. Who doesn't want that?

Stay safe!

Cheers
Bryan

# PSYCHOLOGICAL SAFETY

# Identifying Psychological Warfare

17 November 2020

I expect the term psychological warfare interests you because you are wondering which kind I would be writing about. Would it be about China, the US Election or state border restrictions in Australia? None of those. It's about needing to operate in a culture where psychological safety is not just lacking, it's non-existent.

Recently I invited a guest speaker to my monthly Risk Leadership Group to share her experience in a toxic environment. Let's call her Kate. What Kate experienced was a culture of finger pointing, the blame game and "Don't you dare come to me with anything that might make us look bad!"

Kate's warfare story was about an 18-month period as a senior manager in a governance role in a large organisation. Her boss sat on the executive team and during that time, it became evident that her job was to take care of things so that her boss and the rest of the executive did not need to worry about such things.

It took two weeks for Kate to get her first one-on-one meeting. Over the following months her one-on-ones were cancelled or curtailed with great regularity. By the time her tenure came to an unexpected and abrupt end, she had managed just two hours of face-to-face time with her boss in 18 months.

During that time Kate had done her best to create value in the role that was decidedly not evident when she arrived. While doing so, she soon realised the toxic environment that staff were operating in. So she set about creating psychological safety for her team so they could be more effective in supporting the rest of the organisation. Encouraging them to speak up, to try new approaches and to feel safe in failing.

She then reflected that while she had done the right thing for her team, she had not done the right thing for herself. She did not create psychological safety for herself with her boss and the executive.

How Kate might have achieved this is the topic for my blog next week. In the meantime, why don't you check out this psychological safety checklist from the Bushfire and Natural Hazards Cooperative Research Centre and the University of Tasmania. Then check in next week on how you might tackle a situation where psychological safety does not exist.

Stay safe and build psychological safety!

Cheers
Bryan

# Fighting Psychological Warfare
24 November 2020

Last week I wrote about Kate and her experience of "psychological warfare" (see my blog 'Identifying Psychological Warfare') which is a culture where psychological safety does not exist. Upon reflection, Kate realised that while she created psychological safety for her team she did not create it for herself. So when she spoke up, her boss and others on the executive felt threatened and reacted with an array of avoiding, delaying and blame-shifting strategies.

Kate and I spoke about how she could have done things differently. In hindsight, she realised she needed to confront the situation much earlier and in a very tactful way.

Kate was familiar with my book about creating persuasive conversations, *Persuasive Advising: How to Turn Red Tape into Blue Ribbon*, so we discussed how she might have constructed the conversation with her boss. We agreed that her boss was not aware of the damage that was being caused and how that impacted on her ability to shine. So we focused on a diagram to help explain the situation. Figure 13 is the diagram we came up with.

It shows that staff react to the actions of management based on the emotions stirred in them. And that wrongful actions have impact that fracture the fabric of an organisation's culture. And in seeking safety, staff put up barriers. They don't speak up. They hold on to, even hide, bad news.

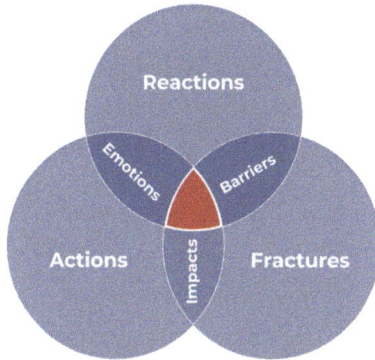

Figure 13: Fighting Psychological Warfare

Diagrams like this work very well as a conversation starter. Something to interest the other person, to demonstrate your deep thinking and to explain what is actually a complex situation.

We agreed that the other element of a persuasive conversation she needed was a story. Why? Because her message would have fallen on deaf ears if her boss was not emotionally ready to hear it. We make decisions on emotion first, logic second, if at all.

Kate had any number of stories of staff literally quivering in their boots and the emotional impact it had on them when interacting with the executive.

So if you want to know the key to winning conversations and the process involved in influencing others i.e. using the Pathfinder Model, I would be pleased to send you a free copy of my ebook. And if you want to go deeper into this, check out my Persuasive Adviser Program.

Stay safe and build psychological safety!

Cheers
Bryan

# P.S. Give Them the WIIFM
1 December 2020

There are more avenues to helping a leader realise they need to change to create psychological behaviour than I shared in my blog last week. While showing them *What was happening* is a good start, you also need to make sure they *Understand what they can have if they make changes*. That is, answer the question "What's In It For Me?" (WIIFM).

A good way to do that is to contrast what is happening now, with the type of changes you are suggesting and the favourable outcomes they can expect. Here are three examples to get you started based on papers written by: Amy Edmondson (the Harvard academic that is widely attributed as having coined the phrase psychological safety)[8]; Bev Attfield, host of the People at Work podcast[9] and Laura Delizonna, executive coach and instructor at Stanford University.[10]

---

8 Edmondson, Amy: *Psychological Safety and Learning Behavior in Work Teams*, Administrative Science Quarterly, 44 (1999): 350-383

9 Attfield, Bev: *7 ways to create psychological safety in your workplace*, Jostle Blog, 2019.

10 Delizonna, Laura: *High-Performing Teams Need Psychological Safety. Here's How to Create It*; HBR, August 24, 2017.

## Focus – Me to Them to Us

There are so many angles to this first one. In essence it is about shifting the focus from what the leader wants to what an individual in the team wants, to ultimately shift the conversation to what the team wants and needs. In doing so, a leader might need to shift their thinking from wanting team members to respect them as the leader, to learning to respect team members more fully for their opinions and actions. Ultimately building a key outcome of trust in one another. An essential element for psychological safety to exist.

## Purpose – Do to Why to What

Everyone, every team, needs a purpose. However, if the leader's focus is on "Do your job" they are missing the point. The more the leader can explain why a team member's job matters in the fulfilment of team and organisational purpose, the sooner the team can start asking the question "What can I do differently to help fulfil our purpose?" This is what Keegan Luiters calls a "questionable purpose" in his book *Team Up*. That is, a purpose statement that can be turned into a powerful question. The example Luiters uses is the British rowing team for the Sydney 2000 Olympics. While their purpose was to win Gold, they translated it into "Will it make the boat go faster?" to guide actions and decisions in the lead up to their one chance to win Gold.

*Everyone, every team,*
*needs a purpose.*
*However, if the*
*leader's focus is on*
*"Do your job" they*
*are missing the point.*

## Conflict – Dissent to Collaborate to Innovate

Conflict is generally never easy. And if the leader you need to influence sees conflict as dissent, a big shift is needed fast. A shift to seeing team members who raise issues in a positive light, will only happen if the team is seen to be collaborative on key issues. The WIIFM for your leader is that teams who collaborate and raise issues will trust each other more and, more likely take risks. And risk taking leads to innovation.

There are many more great outcomes that a team leader can expect if they create psychological safety for their teams. I encourage you to delve into the papers by Edmondson, Attfield and Delizonna. As well, check out what my friend and colleague Dr Amy Silver has written on the topic in her blog Silverlinings. She is known as one of Australia's leading experts on psychological safety.

Stay safe and influence leaders to build psychological safety!

Cheers
Bryan

# Deafening Silence
8 December 2020

While a lack of psychological safety means a team is missing out on the opportunity to take risks and innovate (as I pointed out last week), when the lack of psychological safety becomes rampant, a much bigger risk develops. That risk is the deafening silence that descends on the organisation because no one will speak up. A situation termed organisational or employee silence.

I wrote about this phenomenon a couple of months ago when I reflected on my time at HIH Insurance and the need to sometimes move "Beyond Nudging". In that blog I was encouraging risk practitioners to shift from challenging decisions on a case by case basis to having one big discussion about whether sufficient psychological safety exists. The goal: to create psychological safety so staff in the trenches feel comfortable raising issues, thus preventing many of the decisions that the risk function may need to challenge from ever being made.

It's easy to say that a bigger conversation needs to be had. It's harder to have the conversation if it is not psychologically safe to do so. The Royal Commission noted "... a culture appeared to have developed within HIH not to question leadership decisions."

If you need to have a big conversation, first determine

if the silence is due to explicit or implicit behaviour by management. If explicit, where people are punished for speaking out, you will need to tread very carefully. If it is implicit, where management are not aware of the situation they have created, you will have a slightly easier road.

Either way, you will need to plan your strategy. As I wrote in my book *Persuasive Advising: How to Turn Red Tape into Blue Ribbon*, when delivering bad news, you need to start with **What's great**, move to **What's wrong** while showing plenty of empathy and deliver options for **What's next**. And always finish on a positive.

And as per my Pathfinder Model of persuasion, you will need a powerful story to shift emotions. I have mine. It is the story of Australia's largest corporate collapse, HIH Insurance.

Stay safe and influence leaders to build psychological safety!

Cheers
Bryan

# Dogged Inaction
15 December 2020

Dogged inaction by leaders when staff raise issues is one cause of organisational silence (which I wrote about last week), and ultimately causes the destruction of psychological safety.

Dogged inaction is what happened to the Department of Immigration and Multicultural Affairs around the immigration detention of Cornelia Rau which lead to the 2005 Palmer Report. Rau, an Australian citizen, was illegally detained for ten months. Due to her mental illness her citizenship was not ascertained for all that time.

The beauty of the public sector, *and* a challenge for it, is that when there is a stuff-up, inquiries follow. They provide outstanding opportunities for understanding what went wrong, and why. The Palmer Report described the situation at DIMA as follows:

> *"... the Inquiry found considerable evidence of deafness to the concerns voiced repeatedly by a wide range of stakeholders, a firmly held belief in the correctness and appropriateness of the processes and procedures that exist, and a culture that ignores criticism and is unduly defensive, process motivated and unwilling to question itself. Energies seemed to*

*be channelled more into justifying and protecting the status quo."*

As I wrote last week, you need powerful stories to shift emotions when bringing criticism to leaders. Yes, you can paint them a picture of what is in it for them, but people make decisions on emotion first and logic second. If they are not ready to receive a message containing criticism, you need to prime them with a story. I have gifted you two stories. My personal story of HIH Insurance which is chronicled in the report of the Royal Commission (see last week's blog) and this DIMA one, chronicled in the Palmer Report.

If neither of these stories quite suit your need and you don't have your own, I suggest you go looking for other public inquiries. For example, the inquiry into the Challenger space shuttle disaster in the US or any of the Royal Commissions held in Australia over the last decade. Sadly, there are soooooo many to choose from.

Stay safe and influence leaders to build psychological safety!

Cheers
Bryan

# Withholding Tax
31 May 2022

Taxes are a necessary burden. However, many risk professionals carry an unnecessary burden that is withholding them. The burden of silence.

For any staff member to call something out, or even to voice disagreement with senior leaders, they need to feel psychologically safe to do so. Including risk professionals.

However, being in the position of having to call out a lack of accountability may be an indicator of a different problem. It may simply be that leaders don't see the value in engaging with enterprise risk management. It's your job to show them the value. To "Show them the money!"

How might you do that? That is what my Pathfinder Model of persuasion is for. It is a four-step process:

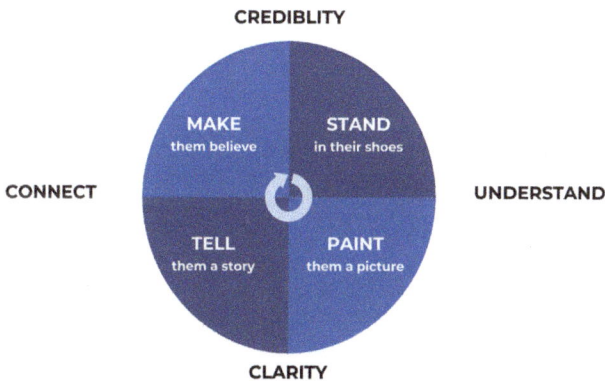

Figure 14: The Pathfinder Model

- **Stand in their shoes** – to understand their problems and how what you do will help to solve them.
- **Paint them a picture** – to provide them with clarity around your solution.
- **Tell them a story** – to bring your solution to life and to help them connect emotionally with you and your solution.
- **Make them believe** – by ensuring you are entirely credible. Have the statistics, case studies and counter arguments all prepared so they are simply convinced.

This four-step process is designed to help navigate the barriers all people put up, to bad or unwanted advice. Next week I will give you an example.

Until then, stay safe and ponder the value ERM brings an organisation!

Cheers
Bryan

# A Conversation

7 June 2022

Last week I promised you an example of my Pathfinder Model in action. I'll do better than that, here's a <u>link</u> to three examples in Chapter 8 in my book *Persuasive Advising: How to Turn Red Tape into Blue Ribbon.* One describes a scenario for a risk professional, another for a finance professional and another for a project management professional.

My Pathfinder Model of persuasion is always my go-to tool when the need to influence someone – or a group – presents itself, and I encourage you to give this a go the next time you find yourself in a similar situation.

Below is a reminder of the four steps to take:

- **Stand in their shoes** – to understand their problems and how what you do will help to solve them.
- **Paint them a picture** – to provide them with clarity around your solution.
- **Tell them a story** – to bring your solution to life and to help them connect emotionally with you and your solution.
- **Make them believe** – by ensuring you are entirely credible. Have the statistics, case studies and

counter arguments all prepared so they are simply convinced.

I trust you will find this useful on your journey to becoming even more persuasive, and that it triggers and develops your own toolkit and intuitive skill that will lead to your success.

Stay safe and remember to practice before you preach.

Cheers
Bryan

# DECISION MAKING

# Modifying your DNA

14 September 2021

No, not yours, your organisation's!

When I engage with senior leaders on their appetite for risk, I talk about embedding it in the DNA of the organisation. Why? Because it is critical for organisational agility.

Decision support tools, like risk assessments, help people make better decisions. However, the key to organisational agility is faster decision making. When a decision maker understands the risk associated with a decision, and they are clear on the organisation's appetite for risk, they can make decisions faster. Including escalating a decision sooner if it sits outside the organisation's current appetite.

In the past, my advice on how to embed your organisation's appetite for risk into the DNA of the organisation, has focused on:

1. Decision maps, and
2. Reviewing and revising your organisation's policies, procedures, processes and systems that guide decision making

These are still critical. However, as you know, not every decision is covered by any one of these.

In training senior leaders – which I wrote about last week – what I have discovered is an increasing willingness for them to take charge of the communication of appetite for risk to their teams. Including time-intensive activities like discussing past decisions or potential decision scenarios over a Lunch and Learn or during a leadership offsite.

There is no doubt that discussions like these help staff develop a better mental model of the decision trade-offs the team needs to make. Inevitably this will deliver better and faster decision making. That is, agility!

Stay safe!

Cheers
Bryan

# Hard Choices

21 September 2021

Hard choices slow us down. Last week I wrote about ensuring staff understand the organisation's appetite for risk to speed up decision making. I have also been heard to say that helping organisations articulate their appetite for risk is one of the hardest things I am asked to do. Why? Because it is hard to express succinctly what are very nuanced considerations for decision making. Often, balancing risk and reward is a hard choice.

In Ruth Chang's TED video 'How to make hard choices' she talks about choices when two alternatives are neither better, worse or equal to the other, she describes them as being "on par". She says that faced with hard choices we often take the safest option.

However, she goes on to say that when there is no obvious best alternative, we can't use rational reasoning to make the right choice. We should use reasons that lie within us for the answer. That is, we should create our own destiny based on our beliefs, our values.

This brings me back to blog after blog I have written about the importance of applying a "value lens" when making tough decisions like ones around risk versus reward. None more important than my one using a pressure cooker analogy to explain how applying a value lens allows organisations to push hard without pushing boundaries that may have adverse consequences years after the event, when uncovered in Royal Commissions, for example.

This year I have helped organisations as diverse as aged care providers, utilities and a not-for-profit in the mental health sector to revise their risk management frameworks and/or their risk appetite statements. Each time I have started from the same point. I ask for a copy of their organisational values.

Stay safe!

Cheers
Bryan

# The Key to Being FaB
3 March 2020

Fab named their washing powder for its "fabulously clean, fabulously fresh and fabulously fragrant" qualities. My use of **FaB** is for **Faster and Better** decision making.

STOP. Don't hang up the phone. You and I know that you and I are great decision makers ... and everyone else has the problem ... right? So. This is not about your decision making. It's about helping THEM. THEM being the people that work for you or the decision makers you are trying to influence.

Fab's Fresh Frangipani has 15 key ingredients, including my personal favourite – Distyrylbiphenyl Disulfonate. Whereas my key to FaB decision making is much simpler. The key is categorisation.

WTF I hear you express. You heard me. CATEGORISATION! Who would have thought? If you don't believe me let's check in with Jeff Bezos. He is the guy that runs that little online bookstore out of Seattle, Washington in the USA. Amazon, I think it is called.

Bezos introduced to Amazon the concept of categorising decisions with Type 1 and Type 2 decisions. Type 2 decisions are reversible. He is very comfortable with his team making these decisions straight out. In fact, he insists on it.

Type 1 decisions he calls "consequential and irreversible or nearly irreversible". That is, they will hurt badly if we don't get them right. Type 1 decisions need to be very well considered. Type 2 decisions can be made much faster.

Does Type 1 and Type 2 decision making sound familiar? Maybe you are thinking of the System 1 and System 2 categorisations made famous by Daniel Kahneman in his book *Thinking Fast and Thinking Slow*. I'll explore this categorisation and how to improve various types of decision making and much, much more in my blogs over the coming weeks.

Cheers
Bryan

# The Key to Being FaB-er
10 March 2020

FaB (Faster and Better) decision making is possible through the right categorisation. Without the categorisation used at Amazon between Type 1 consequential irreversible, and Type 2 reversible decision making that I wrote about last week, we run the risk of either undercooking or overcooking our decision making.

What does this mean? It means that our decision making can be rough when we undercook things. This leads to us constantly needing to rework things. Which in turn leads to us either missing our objectives completely or under achieving them or, at worst, achieving them 6 or 12 months later than we should have. And if we overcook them, we are simply too slow. Delaying achievement of objectives and putting them at risk of being overtaken by external events.

If you categorise well, and improve decision making across the organisation, everything is just smoother. Rework is infrequent and your objectives are achieved 10, 20 or even 30% faster than they otherwise might have been.

And there is more to categorising than simply the Type

*If you categorise well,
and improve decision
making across
the organisation,
everything is just
smoother. Rework
is infrequent and
your objectives are
achieved 10, 20 or
even 30% faster
than they otherwise
might have been.*

1 and Type 2 decisions used in Amazon. In Daniel Kahneman's world of *Thinking Fast and Thinking Slow* his categories are System 1 for fast and System 2 for slow, considered decision making. System 1 is when we use heuristics, little shortcuts to get a quick decision. Such as, assuming a new Italian restaurant down the street will be expensive because the one it's replacing was expensive or because of the way it looks. While that assumption might be wrong, no great harm is done and you have reached a fast decision about whether or not you want to try it sooner or later.

Heuristics are very, very helpful to get us through our day of thousands of decisions. But every now and then they are wrong and they hurt. Like assuming the nice young lad offering to take your car for a car wash to earn a couple of bucks but never bringing it back. (Yep, happened to a friend of mine. The young guy returned two other cars to the workplace before pestering my friend into agreeing to take him up on his car wash service – and of course his car was the most expensive!)

Kahneman and his colleague, Amos Tversky, worked hard to train themselves to identify when thinking fast is not appropriate. They found it difficult. The result? Simply knowing we take shortcuts when we shouldn't is not enough to improve our decision making. We need to put in place interventions.

In my next blog I will talk more on categorisation and on creating those interventions.

Cheers
Bryan

# Observe Within as Much as (With)out
16 June 2020

Observe your team and look for signals from the outside.

Two weeks ago I wrote about the need to diagnose challenges in order to lead. Last week I wrote about the behaviours you are seeing from customers. This week I want you to think about the behaviours you are seeing in your team. There are clues there about the "system". The economy, how the government might act, how the populace might act as our world rapidly changes.

What behaviours do you see? Do you see fear, hubris or something in between? Which of your teams are protecting their patch and who is leaning in? What decisions do they need to make? How are they making them?

The last question is key. A friend of mine shared with me what her colleague, the Chief Health Officer of Victoria (a state in my home country of Australia), recently said:

"Communication is our best strategy against COVID".

What Prof. Brett Sutton is saying is, we need to get into the heads of the populace to influence their decision making. And to judge the effectiveness of the Government's communication and what to do next, requires them to observe the behaviour of people. People in general.

The same applies to you. Observe your team as much as your customers to look for signals as to how your customers and suppliers will be behaving.

Once you have done that, ask yourself, "How can I help them see the decisions that need to be made and to make them?"

Here are my most poignant thoughts on decision making (see my blog 'Working with our tendency for impulsiveness'). They apply now during COVID as much as any other time.

Stay safe and adapt – quickly.

Cheers
Bryan

# Decision Maps
4 May 2021

Decision maps are key to ensuring the right guidance for staff so they can make better decisions, quicker and with more confidence. The result is a more agile organisation. Who doesn't want that?

Anyone who has planned a family trip or tried ordering for a group at a restaurant knows how simple things are if one person has sole authority and makes all the decisions. Add just one more person and it starts getting complicated. Add a couple more and it gets complex. Why? Because people differ in their opinions and, as I wrote about last week, people have different perceptions of risk. In these examples, the risk is that the trip or the meal won't be as enjoyable as expected. Hence the need to ensure adequate guidance for staff to make decisions within the organisation's appetite for risk.

What is a decision map? For an example of one, please have a read of <u>Chapter 8: Appetite for Business</u> from my latest book *Risky Business: How Successful Organisations Embrace Uncertainty*. In essence it is taking an inventory of all the policies, frameworks, processes and systems and determining if they provide sufficient guidance to staff on the organisation's appetite for risk.

A simple example is a check as to whether the financial

*Decision maps are key to ensuring the right guidance for staff so they can make better decisions, quicker and with more confidence. The result is a more agile organisation.*

delegations reflect the organisation's appetite for financial risk.

An example of something that is typically underdone is guidance on innovation. While the organisation's appetite for risk to achieve a specific objective may state that innovation is sought, what policy, framework, process or system sufficiently guides them to take risk within lower and upper boundaries? Both dollar boundaries as well as other boundaries such as environmental sustainability? A decision map can provide sufficient guidance.

If you want to know more about my thoughts on risk appetite <u>download my whitepaper</u> or, better still, <u>buy my book</u> and gain access to my latest risk appetite templates.

Stay safe!

Cheers
Bryan

# AGILITY

# Did Someone Say Agile?

26 July 2022

Recently I was running an education workshop for a group of 35 leaders from a financial services organisation. We looked at their risk culture survey results, their organisation's value statements, the behaviours they see from staff and the behaviours they will need to portray as leaders, to continue to build a strong culture of accountability for the management of risk.

What caught their attention the most was this slide (Figure 15 alongside), when I explained that risk management done well delivers a more agile organisation. One where staff are able to make better decisions, faster, within a sound understanding of the organisation's appetite for risk.

I said to them that I used to say the purpose of enterprise risk management is to build resilience in an organisation. I then asked them: "What makes a small business resilient?" They were a smart bunch, the second suggestion from the audience was "agility". I replied: "Exactly, and that is what Risk Leadership delivers."

I went on to say that Risk Leadership is not leadership by the risk function – although they play a pivotal role. It is about their leadership. Its about risk-based decision making being seen as a leadership imperative. I had their attention and from there the review of culture, values and behaviour was done with vigour.

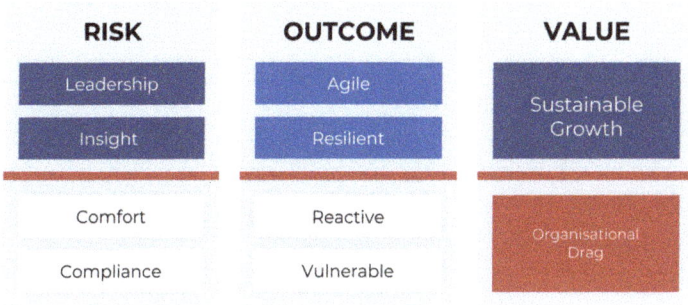

Figure 15: Risk Leadership – A Leadership Imperative

Interestingly the case study we used during the workshop was one of their major IT projects which is being run with the Agile Methodology. My message to them ... the Agile Methodology is a form of risk management. Yes, identify risks and put in a light governance model, but don't overdo it and "throw the baby out with the bath water." It is all about embracing uncertainty, not trying to control it with an iron fist.

For more on embracing uncertainty, I would encourage you to read my latest book *Risky Business: How Successful Organisations Embrace Uncertainty,* including my commentary on the Agile Methodology in the first chapter: An Uncertain World.

Cheers
Bryan

# The Strategy Funnel
23 June 2020

I've taken a sales and marketing tool and turned it into a strategy tool that you might find very helpful right now. The concept works like this:

There are a range of possible futures playing out for each of us. None we can be certain about. The further out in time we look the more uncertain the view. Nothing new here. What is our response? Generally, scenario planning and forecasting. The questions you should be asking yourself now are: "How many scenarios should I be considering?" and, "How can I move them along the strategy funnel?"

The strategy funnel is shown over the page. It starts with scenarios built on the furthest time horizons. Ones with greatest uncertainty and greatest variability between good and bad outcomes. The further down the funnel, the more certainty prevails with the less variability. To start I recommend at least 4 and preferably 6 scenarios. One for each positive and negative scenario, situated at 3 different time horizons.

*The difference between a strategy sales funnel of a year ago, and now, is the shift in time horizons from years to months. The good news about this is, you will know how good your bets were a lot sooner.*

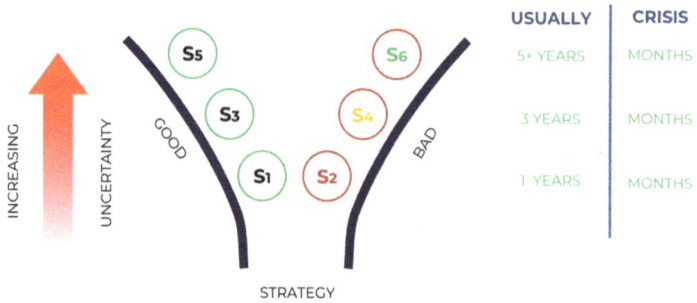

Figure 16: The Strategy Funnel

The difference between a strategy sales funnel of a year ago, and now, is the shift in time horizons from years to months. The good news about this is, you will know how good your bets were a lot sooner.

To set the funnel up for the next 6 months (plus) of COVID, make a record of the main assumptions you have made in each of the scenarios. For example:

- The economy recovers sufficiently; the government decides it does not need to extend the stimulus package beyond September.
- A second wave occurs, and restrictions are reintroduced.
- A second wave occurs and restrictions are not reintroduced; there is a return in large numbers of hospitalisations and multiple fatalities.
- Your competitors reduce/increase prices.
- Consumer confidence improves/remains the same.

Now orientate your strategy to cater for as many of the scenarios as possible or the most likely ones. Both are valid approaches without guarantee of success. Now prepare to move the scenarios through your funnel and reorientate your strategy on say a monthly basis.

In sales and marketing, customers are moved through or out of the funnel via sales and/or marketing contact points. For example: from clicking on an advertisement; to filling out an inquiry form to a call from a sales rep to problem definition, solution and an offer being made. The potential customer can become a customer or exit the funnel at any one of these touch points.

In the case of the strategy funnel, the scenarios are moved through the funnel by asking the question "Was this assumption right or wrong?" If for one particular scenario you are answering "Wrong" often enough, the scenario exits the funnel to be replaced by a new scenario.

I know this might seem like quite a bit of work. However, having a flexible strategy is critical right now. Even more critical is knowing when to re-orientate it. But choose a timeline that makes sense for your business. That might be monthly or quarterly or even longer, especially if you are in a less volatile industry sector.

Stay safe and adapt – quickly.

Cheers
Bryan

# The Strategy Funnel Part II

One of my readers reached out to me after I introduced the strategy funnel last week which made me decide to prepare an example of how the approach works for a prolonged crisis, like COVID-19. One of my sons co-manages the bars in a three-level restaurant offering a variety of dining experiences. It is located in Manly here in Sydney, which is a tourist area. I have been thinking a lot about the restaurants and hence his future. So I thought I would use the restaurant's owners as an example.

A large organisation with a strategy team and/or crisis management team would develop many more scenarios with differing time horizons than I have below, however, to keep this brief, and to make it applicable for a restaurant owner, I only went with two scenarios at the six months horizon.

At the time of writing there are signs of a second wave of the virus occurring in Australia, albeit Victoria is pouring massive resources into combating its outbreaks. In Manly, pubs and restaurants are open but with social distancing restrictions limiting the number of patrons by the 4 sq. m. rule. A number that many might find generally unaffordable if not for government support for wages.

| Scenario 1 – Good 6-month scenario | Scenario 2 – Bad 6-month scenario |
| --- | --- |
| • The Virus – Second wave minimal and controlled. Contact tracing and testing strategy is highly effective. No vaccine available for the foreseeable future.<br><br>• Social Distancing Restrictions – The 4-sq metre restriction capping the number of patrons for inside venues is lifted.<br><br>• The Government (Economy) – Direct financial support to pay employees (JobKeeper in Australia) is not ceased end of September as planned. It is phased out via monthly reductions through to 31 December 2020.<br><br>• The Borders – Interstate borders are fully open. International visitors are welcome but must be tested on arrival and quarantine for 24hrs until test result received.<br><br>• The Public (Economy) – The level of spending stays steady through the back end of 2020.<br><br>• The Public (Health) – The vast majority feel comfortable enough to visit pubs and restaurants. | • The Virus – Second wave occurred and health authorities lost control initially but as spring arrived regained control. No vaccine available for the foreseeable future.<br><br>• Social Distancing Restrictions – Strict social distancing was reintroduced in July and pubs and restaurants were closed again through to November 2020.<br><br>• The Government (Economy) – Direct financial support to pay employees (JobKeeper in Australia) is not ceased end of September as planned. It is phased out via monthly reductions through to 31 December 2020.<br><br>• The Borders – Interstate borders are open between NSW and Victoria all other borders are closed. International visitors remain banned.<br><br>• The Public (Economy) – The level of spending returns to June levels by November 2020.<br><br>• The Public (Health) – A healthy majority of people return to pubs and clubs by November. |

The challenge now is: How do you orientate your strategy?

Again using the restaurant as an example: Can you devise a way of running your business so it can be profitable under both scenarios? For example, can you run a menu set that is cost effective enough, but of sufficient quality to allow you to charge enough to make a profit? Can you get more efficient in your kitchens so you need less staff? Can you centralise some food prep? Can you keep enough reserves in cash to outlast your competitors when government support ends and the industry faces the inevitable rationalisation unless a vaccine becomes available? Can you innovate your business model? For example, developing an at-home fine dining experience using catering equipment and a team of mobile chefs otherwise unemployed?

Once your strategy is set, you need to work hard on it for a month, doing your best not to second guess your assumptions unless something major happens. Then revisit the two scenarios at the end of the month. The scenarios will change or might be completely jettisoned if your assumptions prove very different to the unveiling reality.

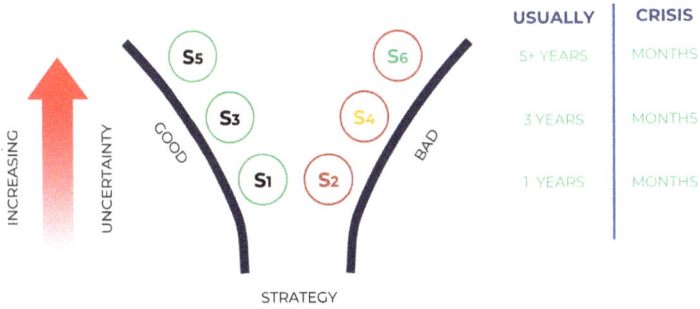

**Figure 17: The Strategy Funnel**

Stay safe and adapt – quickly.

Cheers
Bryan

# What's Coming!

My next book is currently a work-in-progress with the aim of launching it in the first half of 2024.

## TEAM THINK

### How Teams Make Great Decisions

After writing a book about risk-based decision making, *Risky Business: How Successful Organisations Embrace Uncertainty* and one on influencing decision making, *Persuasive Advising: How to Turn Red Tape into Blue Ribbon*, I've embarked on a new challenge. My next book will be called *Team Think* which will uncover the secret to unlocking the collective mind. How to move beyond "two brains are better than one" and on to maximising team performance through enhanced team decision making.

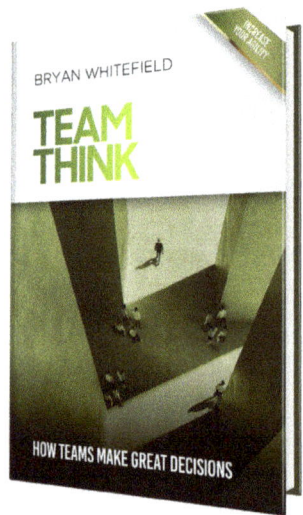

Why does this book need to be written? Because it is for the most part easy to make a decision if you are the only one involved. You and one other party makes it harder.

You plus your team with diverse backgrounds, experience and preferences means it becomes complex.

From strategic decisions, to emerging challenges, to run-of-the-mill board, committee, or team meeting decisions, *Team Think* will demonstrate how your teams can accelerate productivity while avoiding those seemingly innocuous day-to-day decisions that blow up in your face.

*Team Think* will help your teams think bigger together.

To pre-order Team Think go to https://www.bryanwhitefield.com.au/bryans-books/team-think-wait-list/ or via this QR code:

I look forward to you receiving your copy and the conversations that are going to flow as a result.

# Connect with Bryan

Thanks for delving into my book and turning the pages through to the end. I'd love to connect with you further, so below are multiple ways for us to stay connected:

Got questions or want to delve deeper into specific challenges? Feel free to drop me an email at info@bryanwhitefield.com, and my team will find a convenient time for us to **talk**.

If the content you've read here has left you wanting more, consider subscribing to my **blog**, located at the bottom of my website's home page: www.bryanwhitefield.com. It's a great way to stay updated on my insights, tips and resources.

Explore additional resources on my **website** www.bryanwhitefield.com and learn more about my service offering, client testimonials, books, and free resources such as case studies, whitepapers, webinars, tools and templates.

If you want bite-sized videos on a broad range of topics check out my **vlog library** that can be sourced via my You Tube Account https://www.youtube.com/@bryanwhitefield/videos.

And finally, stay connected with me on **LinkedIn** https://www.linkedin.com/in/bryanwhitefield/ as I post daily sharing thoughts, experiences, my IP, research, articles and upcoming events of mine.

www.ingramcontent.com/pod-product-compliance
Lightning Source LLC
Chambersburg PA
CBHW041207220326
41597CB00030BA/5068